FOCUS ON AFRICA

WILDLIFE,

CONSERVATION,

AND

MAN...

FOCUS ON AFRICA wishes to thank the following people, who
share our interest in saving Africa's wildlife, for their generous
assistance and support in the production of this book:

Anya Cristina Stout
Robert R. McComsey
Mark Van Bergh

Published by
Bridgewood Productions Inc.
P.O. Box 50406
Santa Barbara, California, 93150

Library of Congress Catalog Card Number: 93-74178

ISBN 0-9639261-0-1

Printed in Hong Kong

Digital and Print Production by Media 27, Inc., Santa Barbara, California

Focus On Africa

WILDLIFE, CONSERVATION, AND MAN

DAVID S. ANDERSON AND DAVID R. BRIDGE

INTRODUCTION BY DR. RICHARD LEAKEY

DESIGNED AND PRODUCED BY MICHAEL VERBOIS

BRIDGEWOOD PRODUCTIONS, INC.

DEDICATION

On June 2, 1993 a single-engine Cessna airplane piloted by Dr. Richard Leakey, then Director of the Kenya Wildlife Service and world-renowned paleoanthropologist and author, crashed a few miles north of Nairobi. His four passengers miraculously escaped serious injury, but Dr. Leakey himself suffered severe damage to both legs. The timing could hardly have been more excruciating as the Kenya Wildlife Service was on the eve of receiving a $155 million grant from a group of donors led by the World Bank. Despite his injuries, and against all medical advice, he remained in Nairobi so that he could be on hand for the realization of this goal. It was a characteristically courageous decision that cost him dearly. When his doctors warned him that he risked death by further delay, he finally went to England where he lost his right leg below the knee. He soon returned to work in Nairobi, but further misfortune awaited him. By October, he was forced to return to England where his left leg was similarly removed. Following that surgery, he was fitted with prosthetic devices. With his customary grit and good humor, he then embarked on the unexpected task of learning to walk again. It took him just nine days instead of the minimum thirty or forty the doctors assured him would be required. He was back at work by the end of the month.

Following Dr. Leakey's address to the *Focus On Africa* group at Nairobi's Safari Park Hotel on March 26, 1993 he agreed to write an introduction for this book in order to assist the project in its goal—shared with the Kenya Wildlife Service—of helping to conserve Africa's wild heritage. When he was forced to return to England for the second operation, however, he wrote to say that, regretfully, he would be unable to complete that task. His recuperative powers turned out to be greater than he knew, but while the outcome was still in doubt, he agreed to let a transcription of his Safari Park address become the introduction he had intended to write.

This is not the first time he has faced such difficulties, nor is it likely to be the last. In the months following the loss of his legs, he came under vilifying fire from a large group of powerful ministers in the Kenya government. In an effort to resolve the conflict, he offered President Daniel arap Moi his resignation and publicly challenged his critics to show that their motives were other than political. Support poured in from around the world and in March, 1994, President Moi declined to accept his offer. Sadly, this was not to be the end of the story. Dr. Leakey found the redefined conditions under which he was being asked to remain unacceptable. "The Kenya Wildlife Service dream of a self-financing, efficient and effective, publicly owned but independent conservation authority does not seem viable in the context," he said in a statement to the press and submitted his resignation. With that, the light of hope he had so resourcefully kindled for the future of wildlife, not only in Kenya but throughout Africa, dimmed considerably. As he himself put it, the world "will have to wait and see how the Kenya Wildlife Service fares in the future." We of *Focus On Africa* join him in wishing it well.

In the meantime, with regret for this unfortunate outcome and great admiration for his many achievements, we respectfully dedicate this book to Dr. Richard Leakey.

CONTENTS

WELCOME TO AFRICA

As a Kenyan, and especially as a Kenyan responsible for wildlife management and conservation in this country, I was particularly pleased to see a group such as *Focus On Africa* that did not just travel around the continent, but also took some time to see what we're trying to do. We want people to see that the country is not all that the press says it is in terms of insecurity and crises. Once you get away from the big cities and the political turmoil of the hubs, the wilderness areas of this country are pretty much as they've always been and in some respects you can do pretty much what you've been able to do for many, many years. This is not to say that everything we're doing is right or that everything we're doing today we'll be doing tomorrow. There are opportunities to make some very dramatic changes.

Focus On Africa came at a time of transition in every sense of the word. It's not my purpose here to address the subject of the political and economic transition that is taking place, but I can say that a trip to Kenya, if you're paying in foreign currency, is a lot cheaper now than it was a short time ago. Obviously, the devaluation should do us a lot of good. My hope to the tour operators and hoteliers is, let's not once again kill the goose that is laying the golden egg by pushing up prices to take unnecessary advantage of devaluation. The cheap shilling is a boon, I believe, and should help us make an enormous difference.

The Kenya Wildlife Service represents something new in a Third World country. Unlike virtually all other countries, we expect to make conservation pay for itself. When I took over nearly four years ago, Kenya wildlife management was receiving one-hundred percent of its funding from the central government, which reflected treasury support through taxpayer revenue. Kenya has a relatively small tax base. Taxes are high for the few who pay them and it's not elastic. We had reached the point where it was virtually impossible to see how wildlife management could receive any larger slice of the cake, given the other priorities that government had to set—health, education, security, agriculture, and so forth. We were looking at a situation where one could predict a deteriorating return. It was for that reason that the government moved to establish the wildlife service as a publicly owned corporation to operate, as do other corporations in this country, with the facility to keep all the money that we raised. The fee you pay to enter a national park goes directly to the Kenya Wildlife Service and is applied directly to the management of wildlife. It doesn't get offset against the national priorities where, out of every dollar that used to be paid, wildlife might have gained a couple of cents. Today, for every dollar paid, a dollar goes to the wildlife corporation and is used specifically for wildlife in the broadest sense.

I say in the broadest sense because obviously we are concerned with poaching, and we've dealt with that. We are concerned with some of the infrastructural needs and we're dealing with those. But we have to see wildlife in the context of the country. It is not an isolated sector. It operates as part of the national economy. Conservation is a strategic issue as far as we're concerned. But more importantly, wildlife lives on land that, at one time, belonged to somebody. All the peoples of Kenya moved across their respective areas and just because not many people happened to be living in the areas where national parks were set up doesn't mean that they didn't sense some ownership. So there is a problem of land alienation and it is our intention to try to redress that alienation by giving something back. Most of the wildlife would not survive in the national parks if the parks were constrained by hard boundaries.

When the national parks were first established in this country, it was assumed that the wildlife could continue to wander land that was inhabited by pastoral nomads because pastoral nomads would remain pastoral nomads forever. There was no sense that this land might one day have other uses. So places like the Masai Mara, Amboseli, to a certain extent Tsavo and some of the other parks, are core areas and the wildlife spends fifty to sixty percent of its time beyond the boundaries of the parks, grazing and feeding on land that is today seen as private or

communal land. Obviously, it competes with sheep and goats and people trying to farm, but unless the wildlife can continue to wander, there will not be viable national parks. To redress that issue, we are setting aside a significant proportion of our funds to support community projects. Twenty-five cents on the dollar goes to a community welfare fund that is being used to build schools and provide scholarships for every student level from preschool to university. We are also providing clean water, veterinary medicine, medical clinics and all manner of other things that these communities need. As a consequence, many of these rather desperate areas are beginning to see the wildlife as something much more important than they ever dreamed because there is a real return from the tourist activity and they can see the benefit of sustaining the parks by letting the wildlife move across their land.

There has been a very positive and constructive change in the last year and a half. A lot of people feel somewhat guilty about the poverty they see around the parks and wonder what is being done for the other problems of Kenya. We are trying to integrate the two together. When I say that all the money tourists pay to enter the park is going to wildlife, obviously a school or clinic isn't wildlife, but if it's a school or clinic adjacent to a park, it's a very important part of the wildlife issue. By 1994, government will provide none of our finance. We have moved in four years to a complete private enterprise approach with no taxpayer support. This is a very risky road to be on. Fortunately, the government saw the wisdom of it and, in the first three years of our existence, our budget quadrupled despite the fact that government funding went down to less than five percent.

One of the concerns visitors have when they go out to the parks, and one of ours as well, is that in many cases there are far too many people going to far too few areas. Often they find vehicles crowding around what they're trying to photograph and they get rightfully irritated. They see that many visitors are being driven around by less than courteous guides who will drive across their photo view or get behind the animals and spoil the backdrop of Kilimanjaro or one of the other spectacles here. We would like to see more tourists come because, as we improve the infrastructure, we really need more revenue and more revenue probably means more people. But they must be spread out. At the moment, something like ninety percent of our visitors are going to less than seven of fifty-two protected areas. So there is enormous scope for increasing the number of visitors while decreasing the number in any one area. This is something that will be addressed very seriously in the coming year.

We also recognize that bouncing around in a vehicle is not the best way to see wildlife and that sometimes people would like to get out and spend a little time closer to nature or to travel in a vehicle that is more open as they do in other parts of Africa. We are exploring this.

We believe ecotourism is more than being cooped up in a closed vehicle where you can stand up in the hatch, but you can't do much else. But we must provide safety. It's no good saying you can get out of the car if the first thing that happens is you get eaten. That would be cause for legitimate negative publicity about Kenya. We are working with the private sector, exploring training opportunities and certification so that certain guides will be able to carry out ecotourist activities. This would relate to areas of the country where you might go if you had a blue chip guide as opposed, say, to a silver chip guide. We can use market forces to control numbers. Many very innovative ideas are being explored that I believe will add considerably to the attraction and value of what is being done here.

We used to be concerned about the poaching problem. We were losing elephants in Kenya at the rate of three or four thousand a year. The elephant population went from sixty-five or seventy thousand down to eighteen thousand in fifteen years. The rhinos went from eighteen thousand to two or three hundred. This was an impossible situation to sustain and fortunately we've been able to bring it under control. We lost perhaps twenty-two elephants and no rhino last year. This has nothing to do with a tough wildlife force armed with guns and efficiency; it has to do with the fact that the world community stopped buying ivory for baubles and trinkets. There has been a social/political movement in North America and Europe, now spreading to Japan, that has made it antisocial to wear wild animal products such as ivory. The effect of that, perhaps stimulated by the ivory bonfire to some small degree, has been to push down demand and thus, to push down the price. When we burned the ivory in 1986, it was $300 a kilo or $150 a pound. Today, ivory is selling—if you can sell it—for about $5 a pound on the Kenya black market. If you drop the price to $5 a pound and increase the risks substantially, people aren't going to go after elephants. It's no longer a problem as far as we're concerned.

It could come back if the price comes back and the price will come back if people start buying ivory again because someone tells them, it's okay...this is legal ivory. Consumers don't understand such details. They like to be led, and ivory is either okay or it's not. If it's not okay, most won't touch it. If it is okay, they're not going to ask questions; they will assume that whoever is selling it to them knows what they're doing. We are therefore concerned about efforts in Zimbabwe to reopen the ivory trade because we don't believe we can control it and if we can't control it, with the multi-million dollar project we've got going here, most African countries won't be able to control it either and the elephants will go. I don't think there's any question about that.

Zimbabwe claims that halting the ivory trade has put them into poverty and that they can no longer manage their wildlife because they don't have the money for it. However, if they raised the price of entry to their national parks by $1.50 they could recoup all of the money they're losing through not selling ivory.  Zimbabwe's parks are among the cheapest in the world. Most of the traveling public are nature lovers and environmentalists and $1.50 today doesn't buy a poor quality white wine on a U.S. domestic flight if you're traveling economy. I would think that most of us could afford to contribute that amount of money to keep the elephants off the endangered list.

Kenya has an enormous number of parks and protected areas of which you only get to see a few. I am sure visitors will have some sense that things could be better, whatever they see. We need to open up those other areas and this costs money. We need roads, camps, security. The infrastructural changes that are necessary, we project, will cost close to $150 million. That's a lot of money and it couldn't be raised locally. But we've been fortunate. We've raised $148 of the $150 million. All sorts of road projects are underway so that we can get these places open. Within the next year or year and a half, tour operators and safari guides will be able to take tourists to any number of destinations that are not currently available.

It seems to me that the *Focus On Africa* program was mounted with a great deal of imagination and vision. At a time when many people are avoiding Kenya, I wanted to add my voice to those who said, welcome, and thanks for looking a little farther than the tabloids and the alarmist reports. Yes, we have problems, but they're not that bad. Come, see it and judge for yourselves.

Dr. Richard Leakey
former Director of the Kenya Wildlife Service

On the lush green floor of Ngorongoro Crater, a solitary black rhinoceros stands in the tall grass watching a storm roll across the crater's rim. Only a scant handful of his relatives still live in this place where once there were many. It is the same everywhere in Africa. Their horns, designed for defense, became instead the instrument of their doom and now they are almost gone. Watching that lone rhino face the storm, it is hard not to imagine that he is, in his own dim way, aware of all this. But if not, we are certainly aware of it. He and his struggle to survive brought us here—not, as so often in the past, to steal his life, but to offer him a helping hand. Standing there like some huge living boulder, waiting for the rain, he seems to embody the whole tragedy of Africa. I think of a child's question from long ago: If we had only one tear, what would we cry for?

David R. Bridge

Wildlife, Conservation, & Man

The problem with wildlife in Africa—and everyone agrees that there is one, even if they can't always agree on what to do about it—begins and ends with man. In 1909, when Theodore Roosevelt came to hunt big game, estimates of Africa's human population stood at 118 million. In just under eighty years it soared to nearly 700 million. If growth should continue at that rate, in another eighty years the population would reach 1.3 billion. According to some recent studies, however, the pace appears to be slowing—perhaps dramatically. If true, it's certainly good news for Africa and its beleaguered wildlife. As we've seen in the long agony of Ethiopia, Sudan and Somalia, the continent has had great difficulty supporting even its present population. How could it possibly sustain 1.3 billion and, more to the point, its wildlife at the same time?

The wildlife may never have equalled these enormous human numbers, but in Roosevelt's time it certainly seemed inexhaustible—just as it had in mid-19th century America. Unfortunately, this impression of inexhaustibility proved as illusory in Africa as it had in America. There, after centuries of living in balance with the Indians whose way of life depended on them, the buffalo herds that once blackened America's "sea of grass" were slaughtered to the brink of extinction in less than fifty years by the white man. Viewed from today's perspective—vastly different from that of the late 19th century— the destruction of those buffalo herds and our brutal treatment of the Indians appear shocking and deplorable, by far the darkest chapter in American history. But regardless of how inexcusable it may seem in retrospect, the United States would have found it well-nigh impossible to pursue its "manifest destiny to overspread the continent allotted by Providence for the free development of our multiplying millions" without displacing both the buffalo herds and the Indian tribes that depended on them. There may have been a better, more humane way to accomplish this objective, but neither the government in Washington nor the pioneers moving west gave a fig about that at the time.

Today we no longer consider such 19th century-style solutions acceptable. As present-day Africa struggles with conflicts between man and wildlife, it doesn't have the luxury of doing so in private as America did. The world community watches with sharpening interest, ready to intercede (or meddle, depending on how you look at it). Huge though it may be, the continent's natural resources, including good farmland, are not as abundant as they might be. As British writer Alan Moorehead once observed, the African ark is running out of room.

Ironically, the notion of conservation as policy found vigorous life and expression in the mind of the very same Theodore Roosevelt who stalked those *African Game Trails* back in 1909, blazing away at everything he could get his sights on. Indeed, he did more for the cause of conservation than any other American president before or since. America's National Park concept, born at Yellowstone in 1872 and strongly supported by Roosevelt, eventually encircled the earth. In Africa, it reached some very impressive dimensions: Tanzania's Serengeti, 5,698 square miles; South Africa's Kruger National Park, 7,719; Kenya's Tsavo, 8,053 (roughly the size of Massachusetts); Zambia's Kafue, 8,648; Namibia's Namib/Naukluft and Etosha National Parks, 9,116 and 8,595 respectively. These six parks alone comprise 47,829 square miles of land—an area almost exactly the size of Mississippi, or 0.24 percent of the entire surface of the earth. Yellowstone, America's largest National Park at 3,472 square miles, is slightly smaller than Puerto Rico.

Size, of course, is only one criterion. America's parks were created primarily to save uniquely scenic areas, but in Africa protecting wildlife was the main objective. Except to those who revel in wide open spaces, the flat expanse of the Serengeti Plain can hardly be described as scenic. Nevertheless, like many of Africa's great national parks, it contains a rich and varied fauna. The pastoral Maasai, like the North American Plains Indians, had lived on the Serengeti in harmony with the wildlife for untold generations when the white men arrived and immediately began behaving the same way they had in North America. In a remarkably short time, they transformed the face of the continent and its entire ecology. Of course, ecology as a science was unknown at the time, as was the notion that we had any responsibility to protect creatures other than ourselves. When the idea of conserving wildlife, which had been disappearing at an alarming rate, finally dawned on the colonialists, it was predictably the Maasai and other indigenous cultures who paid the price. In 1958, the Maasai were obliged to sign an agreement they couldn't even read that committed them to vacating the Serengeti. Later, they were evicted from Ngorongoro Crater and Amboseli when those areas became national parks. In Africa, the natives were thrown off the reservations instead of herded onto them. With this, the pattern of separating the animals' fate from that of the local people was set. It was a policy that would ultimately prove disastrously short-sighted.

Before the colonial powers came, nationalism, with all its attendant problems, rivalries, central governments and political turbulence, was unknown. African tribes lived in harmony with nature, if not necessarily with each other. The influence of the colonialists, with their missions and clinics, helped to trigger the population explosion of this century. The result of that explosion has been no less a disaster for the Africans than the wildlife. Twenty years ago, Peter Matthiessen wrote in *The Tree Where Man Was Born*: "In Tanzania, intensive agriculture is seen as the solution to malnutrition and unemployment, and a population increase is encouraged. But except in the highlands, the red earths of East Africa are too poor to support permanent agriculture, and where they are fertile, the soils are soon impoverished by the plow, which lays them bare to cycles of fierce sun and leaching rain. In the wet season the ground is muck, and in the dry a hard-caked dusty stone." With its shortage of natural resources and the dubious distinction of possessing twenty-nine of the world's thirty-six poorest countries, Africa has limited options for generating foreign exchange. Chief among these is its wildlife. Tourists come from all over the world just to see it 'and, until recently, there was also a wide-open international market for wildlife and wildlife products: ivory, rhino horn, leopard and cheetah skins, primates for research labs, and of course, animals for the world's zoos.

In the new age of environmentalism, however, traffic in these products hasn't been quite the free and open proposition it used to be. The international community, after a protracted and often acrimonious debate, finally agreed in 1989 to place the elephant on Appendix I of the Convention on International Trade in Endangered Species (CITES) which effectively shut down the ivory trade. The supply of rhino horn, much prized in the Orient for its alleged medicinal and love-enhancing properties and in some Arab countries for carving into dagger handles, dwindled with the enormous toll taken on the rhino population by poachers. Wearing wild animal skins is no longer considered fashionable or politically correct. And finally, the traffic in primates for laboratories has come under mounting pressure from animal rights groups. Nowadays, they're more apt to show up in native markets where a live chimpanzee, for example, might sell as meat for the local equivalent of eight or ten dollars.

In the 1980s, a firestorm of protectionist emotion engulfed the international ivory trade and the havoc it was reportedly wreaking among the elephant population. Poaching—particularly in places like Kenya's immense Tsavo National Park, which was to become darkly symbolic of the whole problem—burst out of control. The press, ever sensitive to the temper of the times, treated its readers to a parade of horror stories about the brutal slaughter, often accompanied by gruesome photographs of elephant corpses with their faces and feet hacked off. Aroused by this grisly carnage, sentiment for an international ban on the ivory trade gradually rose to fever pitch. The furor reached its apogee at an unprecedented and eye-popping event in the fall of 1989 when Kenya, guided by Richard Leakey, ostentatiously burned twelve tons of ivory in Nairobi National Park, at a cost to the country of some three-million dollars in lost revenues. It may have been wasteful as some critics charged (after all, the elephants were already dead), but the sheer spectacle of such a conflagration and the worldwide press coverage it received probably did more to accomplish the objective than any other single act. After years of bickering, the ban was finally imposed in October 1989 and remains in force to this day.

Lately, pressure has been building against it, particularly among the southern African nations who claim that the ban brought economic hardship and deprived them of the revenue necessary to conserve wildlife. Conservation organizations have launched major lobbying campaigns to keep it in place. Once again, the argument seems likely to be long and heated. Economics pitted against the sympathetic emotion elephants are able to generate in the public mind—two enormously powerful forces contending in a volatile and troubled continent. Can elephants be managed as a renewable resource? At the moment, the public at large, particularly in the Western world where the money is, doesn't seem quite ready to accept such a notion. Richard Leakey opposes lifting the ban because he does not believe the ivory traffic can be controlled. Poaching, he argues, became a crisis precisely because the price of ivory, fed by international demand, had skyrocketed to $150 a pound. With the imposition of the ban, demand evaporated and the price fell to $5 a pound on the black market. In today's ever more crowded world, however, wildlife must earn its keep and ivory is undeniably one way for elephants, who otherwise exert so much destructive pressure on the land, to do that. It has been a significant African resource for centuries. The economic pressure to reinstate the trade isn't likely to abate, so the problem of how to insure survival of the elephants seems likely to be with us for a long time.

Meanwhile, political events in various parts of Africa and the press's often sensational coverage of them combined to depress the flow of visitor traffic that gives wildlife its greatest economic value. When tourists themselves came under assault by local bandits in some of the parks (Tsavo was again at the center of this dismal development and vehicles crossing from Tsavo to Amboseli were still required to carry an armed ranger at the time of the *Focus on Africa* safaris), the travel business suffered a grievous blow. If prospective visitors felt in fear for their very lives, less risky and expensive destinations would soon siphon them away. And so it proved. In 1991, Kenya had 804,600 visitors, but in 1993 that number dropped sharply. By the time the first wave of the 136 amateur and professional photographers of the *Focus On Africa* project arrived in March of that year, a page-one story in the *Nairobi Standard* reported that air passenger traffic had declined by a staggering 70%. Of course, scare stories in the press weren't entirely responsible for this development; a shaky world economy no doubt played an even larger role. Nevertheless, the consequences for Africa's wildlife of such a decline, if protracted, will be serious. From the perception of that threat, *Focus On Africa* was born.

Michael Verbois, former Vice President of Brooks Institute of Photography in Santa Barbara and an ardent Africa enthusiast, and David Anderson Safaris began exploring various ways to boost tourism and help the wildlife. Over the next several months, *Focus On Africa* began to take shape. Mike, who had been involved in a project called *Focus On New Zealand* a few years before, suggested applying its basic concept of using amateur and professional photographers to capture the safari experience in pictures that could then be published in a high quality book. It was agreed to make the project's objective the conservation of Africa's wildlife through the promotion of tourism—a sound idea as far as it went, but the problem was soon revealed to be much more complicated and controversial than it appears on its face.

For one thing, tourism as the principle route toward the salvation of wildlife has come under increasing fire from environmental groups lately. They claim, with some justice, that too many tourists are worse than too few; that hordes of tourists and their vehicles disrupt the animals' natural behavior patterns and destroy their habitat with off-road excursions. Richard Leakey once observed that, thanks to constant stalking by armies of picture-taking tourists, the cheetah "no longer lives like a wild animal." Well, perhaps. It can certainly be argued that uncontrolled and poorly managed tourism is more a part of the problem than the solution, but without tourism the future of Africa's wildlife would be extremely bleak, if not completely hopeless. The solution, if there is one, must be more than just tourism; it must be *responsible* tourism. But exactly what does that mean? How can it be implemented and with whom does the responsibility lie?

"I had a farm in Africa," Isak Dinesen began in her most famous book, *Out of Africa*, and with those words she managed to convey something at once haunting and hypnotic about the allure of this continent. So potent was this peculiar magic that when it became a 1985 movie with Robert Redford and Meryl Streep, the annual stream of visitors to Kenya soared from 300,000 in 1983 to nearly 800,000 by 1990. To this day, guides point out with obvious pride locations where particular scenes were filmed. In a very real sense, a safari is like returning to the place where man was born— where the natural world is the *only* world. Nowhere else do we feel the joy of being alive quite so keenly. Nowhere else does the meaning of being human seem quite so elemental or so awesome.

For many who have had long-standing fantasies about going to Africa, actually making the trip seems like the impossible dream. But what if that could be changed? Would the magic of Africa be contagious? Would others share these feelings about the land, the people and, most of all, the animals? Could that contagion be effectively and responsibly harnessed to the cause of conservation and if so, how? To launch *Focus On Africa*, David Anderson Safaris designed twenty-five itineraries to eight countries from Kenya to South Africa. The help and participation of numerous hotels, lodge and camp owners, tour operators, guides, airlines, and a handful of U.S. concerns who agreed to assist in various ways were enlisted. To attract as many people as possible, the safaris were offered at a substantial discount in exchange for which the participants agreed to make their photographs available for publication in the book. The response exceeded all expectations.

Clearly, the bookstores had no shortage of spectacular (and expensive) books on Africa, its people and its wildlife. Most are the work of professional photographers who spend years living in the field with their subjects. The results obtained by photographers like Jonathan Scott (*The Leopard's Tale*), Reinhard Künkel (*Elephants*), and Frans Lanting (*Okavango*) are indeed heart stopping and unforgettable, but few people can hope to imitate their achievements. For the vast majority, seeing one of their photographs published in such a glossy book seems about as likely as climbing Mt. Everest or winning $50 million in the lottery. But suppose, while browsing through a bookstore, you came upon a book full of pictures taken not just by professionals, but by people with little more photographic experience than yourself. Would it, perhaps, inspire you to get involved in the conservation effort by participating in ecotourism? Confronted daily with an array of seemingly intractable world problems, most of us feel powerless to do anything about them, but this might be a way to change that and have the time of your life into the bargain. There was no evidence that such a concept had been tried before and the wildlife's need for help made it almost a duty for those of us who care about such things to try.

In Swahili, the word *safari* means journey. Of course, no one thinks of taking a safari to Chicago (regardless of how "wild" the life there might be); the term has become synonymous, not with travel in general, but specifically with a trip into the African bush in search of game. Since Teddy Roosevelt's day, the world has shrunk. It took him twenty-nine days to get from New York to Mombasa by ship. Today's traveler covers the same distance by jet in about fifteen hours. Even with a generous allowance for airline delays and other unforeseeable interruptions, it's like warp speed by comparison. Roosevelt, ever the advocate of the strenuous life (he once insisted on finishing a campaign speech despite the minor inconvenience of having been shot by a would-be assassin) and freshly relieved of the burdens of the presidency, came with his son Kermit and a host of others to bring down some mighty beasts of the field—ostensibly for the scientific collections of Washington's Smithsonian Institution. In the process, he probably launched the great age of African safaris.

The logistical support required for Roosevelt's expedition staggers the late 20th century imagination. Any present-day safari seems puny by comparison. As Roosevelt himself described it, "...our preparations were necessarily on a very large scale; and as we drew up at the station the array of porters and of tents looked as if some small military expedition was about to start. As a compliment, which I much appreciated, a large American flag was floating over my own tent; and in the front line, flanking this tent on either hand, were other big tents for the members of the party, with a dining tent and skinning tent; while behind were the tents of the two hundred porters, the gun bearers, the tent boys, the askaris or native soldiers, and the horse boys or saises." With respect to Roosevelt's mission to collect specimens, times have also changed. If he arrived in Kenya today, he wouldn't be allowed to bag a single Thomson's gazelle, let alone the 512 elephant, rhino, buffalo, leopard, cheetah and assorted other game from hyraxes to shrews he and Kermit alone dispatched in their year-long safari. Kenya banned hunting in 1977 and even in other parts of Africa where it is still permitted, it's strictly controlled and quite costly. It's done, not in the parks, but on private game reserves and land concessions granted to various hunting companies by governments and private owners. Most of today's visitors are more interested in bringing back memorable photographs than trophies to mount in museums or on the billiard room wall.

The world offers many potentially unique experiences, depending on how flexible your personal definition of that word happens to be, but perhaps none quite like an African safari. Diminished though it may be, it's still the last great wildlife show on earth. Most of the animals here can be found nowhere else and certainly nowhere in such variety and abundance. Not since the buffalo herds roamed North America has there been anything to compare with the annual wildebeest migration. Some two-million strong and mingled with legions of zebra, it flows across the Serengeti Plain like a tide. How can we insure that it, too, doesn't vanish in a sad reprise of yesteryear's folly? Must the lion, leopard and cheetah go the way of the timber wolf, grizzly bear and cougar—all substantially exterminated over large parts of their former range? Will the rhinos, one of our last remaining links to the astounding megafaunas of bygone eras, disappear forever merely because their horns are falsely believed by some to cure illness or enhance sexual desire? Can the elephants, who do so much unwitting damage to trees and farmers' crops, be preserved, not just for future generations to marvel at as we do, but for their own sakes?

These are deeply perplexing questions. Only in the latter part of this century have we finally begun to realize that the dominion over the earth and all its creatures conferred upon us by the Bible carries heavy responsibilities that we have been sorely neglecting. Somehow, the value of this wildlife resource must find its way down to the local populations who have been forced to give up their land for it and who still have to live with it and its inevitable depredations on a daily basis. Peter Matthiessen put it this way: "The parks for which their lands have been appropriated, and which they themselves have no means to visit even if they were interested, give sanctuary to marauding animals that are a threat to domestic stock and crops, not to speak of human life, and their resentment is natural and just. It is no good telling a shamba dweller that tourist revenues are crucial to the nation when his own meager existence remains unaffected, or is affected for the worse. Even the urban African benefits little from a tourist economy, not to speak of the revenues from the parks, which are resented as the private preserves of white foreigners and the few blacks at the top." Regrettably, little has changed in the twenty years since Matthiessen wrote that. What *has* changed, of course, is our level of awareness and, hence, our concern about ecological issues. Even so, environmentalism remains an indulgence only the more affluent countries can afford, regardless of what long-term local and even world-wide consequences may result from ignoring it everywhere else.

Tourism may not be the only solution to the wildlife conservation problem, but it is an indispensable part of any solution because, in the main, wildlife's economic value consists of its power to draw tourist dollars. That very fact, however, creates a modern conundrum: If too little tourism diminishes wildlife's value and too much threatens to overwhelm and destroy it, how can we find a viable balance that will both save the animals and serve the people? As with so many issues where money and power are at stake, this one has become a political football, booted about by governments, rivalrous conservation organizations and an alphabet soup of environmental and animal rights groups that have too often shown little regard for the role that will have to be played by the local populations.

The momentum of history finally appears to be flowing in a more favorable direction. After centuries of virtually heedless exploitation of the earth and its natural resources, we now have the opportunity and, apparently, the will to make a major change in our attitudes and actions. It may be our last such opportunity. If we fail and the environmentalists' darkest predictions come true, future generations will surely inherit a planet deprived of large parts of its natural heritage. Our capacity to regret such a loss is one of the things that sets us apart from the rest of the animal world.

Having created the problem, we alone have the power to do something about it.

At the conclusion of the twenty-five *Focus on Africa* safaris, we asked the participants to fill out a questionnaire regarding their personal views and experiences. We asked: "What feelings and thoughts did you have about Africa before your safari?

"Hot, humid, dirty, smelly, rough and unsophisticated, dangerous, hard to get around in."

—Drew Horton

"The Dark Continent, sleeping in tents, hot and dusty, never-ending bumpy roads."

—Kathy Gregg

"Uncivilized, dangerous, jungle, Tarzan, lions, excitement."

—Sharon Hackley

"It was a place I had never been and had no desire to go. It was where Somalia was and was full of famine, cannibals and mosquitoes. I also saw an A&E special on how tourism was destroying Kenya. It was gross."

—Michael Sheras

"Dry, dusty lands. Somewhat harsh and arid scenery. Over-populated."

—Karen McGougan

"A long way; very different; an 'unknown' continent with little information generally available compared to Europe or Asia; a strange place for an American to take a vacation."

—Mark Van Bergh

For those with such views and apprehensions, the actual experience proved more than a little edifying. Naturally, the next question was: "What words describe your feelings and thoughts now that you've returned from your African safari?" Here's how those same people filled that one out:

"Africa is the most unique, beautiful, special and magical place I've ever been. I felt as if I had been there before. I am now dedicated to doing what I can to help conserve Africa's environment, cultures, and wildlife."

—Drew Horton

"Excellent accommodations, abundant wildlife in natural settings, magnificent birds, extremely knowledgeable and friendly guides, cold and dusty."

—Kathy Gregg

"Beautiful, friendly, wild, dusty, absolutely delightful."

—Sharon Hackley

"It was a wonderful place. The people were friendly everywhere and the scenery and animals were great. The weather was wonderful and the mosquitoes non-existent."

—Michael Sheras

"Green, gentle rolling beautiful countryside. Large wide-open spaces. Sparsely populated outside the cities."

—Karen McGougan

"An easier place to travel than people tend to think; one of the best, if not the best, vacations; some of the friendliest people; some of the most beautiful landscapes around; a fascinating look at different cultures which reminds you that we're all part of the same world and that differences among people and cultures should be appreciated, not feared."

—Mark Van Bergh

Even in this age of instant global communications, American misconceptions about Africa remain widespread. Unfortunately, reports that make it into the international press often deepen rather than relieve the problem. On August 1, 1993, less than a month after our safaris came to an end, the *Los Angeles Times* ran an article that began, "Kenya Beefs Up Security For Tourists: Kenya, its tourist trade hurt by banditry and rubbish in game parks, is counterattacking by cleaning up trash, beefing up security forces and wooing big spenders." It went on to say, "The troubles began in 1988 when a British tourist was murdered under still-unexplained circumstances in Masai Mara game park, 120 miles south of Nairobi. German, American and British tourists were persistently attacked in game parks between May and November of last year, Kenyan officials said, and a Kenyan driver was shot and injured when bandits attacked Dutch tourists near the Masai Mara last month." The article also stated that tourism revenues had dropped from $400 million in 1991 to $295 million in 1992. Overlooked in such media alarums is the indisputable fact that you're safer every day in almost any part of Africa, politically troubled or otherwise, than you would be on the streets of most major American cities after dark.

But unfortunately, scary headlines and tales of death and danger sell more newspapers.

The damage likely to result from such intimidating stories may seem slight to the casual observer, but tour operators know better. A week before the story quoted above appeared, David Anderson Safaris ran an expensive ad in the *Los Angeles Times*. Afterward, the staff spent most of their time trying to assuage callers' fears about the dangers of travel in Africa rather than booking them for safaris. No one would suggest that the press falsify or dilute its coverage of these events for the benefit of the tourist business. The public certainly has a right to know what's going on, especially in areas of the world where travel may entail some risks. It's a question of balance. The British tourist murdered under mysterious circumstances in 1988 was Julie Ward, a young woman traveling alone, whose disappearance received international attention because her father made such heroic efforts to find her. She was one of 694,000 visitors to Kenya that year, but this relevant fact doesn't show up in the story. Nor does the article say how many German, American and British tourists were "persistently attacked" in 1992, or with what consequences. No death or injury should be viewed as trivial. Still, an average of 2.8 homicides occurred *every day* in Los Angeles during 1991— more than a thousand killings, the majority of which probably went unnoticed by the general public or even the *Los Angeles Times*. Families bound for a vacation at Disneyland might experience some anxiety as a result of reading about the city's routine violence and crime, but they wouldn't be likely to cancel their trip on that account. Africa is easier to avoid because it's far away and expensive to get to. Since life is an endless series of calculated risks, we naturally tend to avoid the ones that seem greater, whether they really are or not.

But what about the environmentalists' complaint that too many tourists are destroying rather than saving the wildlife and its habitat? In the last twenty years, we have been regularly assaulted with apocalyptic forecasts concerning the destructiveness of man. The cumulative effect of all this handwringing and doomsaying has been, at best, depressing, and at worst, downright misleading. We're still waiting for a final verdict on most of the cataclysmic predictions about ozone holes, greenhouse effects, silent springs and the like. The decibel level of these dark forecasts no doubt results from our belief that it's only the public perception of crisis that generates action. These crises may or may not ultimately prove to have substance. Still, there can be little doubt that uncontrolled and reckless tourism does result in damage to national parks (in Africa or anywhere) as well as to the animals that live in them and the cause of conservation as a whole. All this has given rise in recent years to a new concept called "ecotourism," roughly defined as tourism with an ecological conscience. Is it real, or just another gimmick cooked up by the travel industry to get people traveling?

Much debate swirls with mounting intensity around that question these days. Are we, as so many environmentalists would have us believe, teetering on the edge of a bottomless precipice? Will life on earth become untenable if we fail in our responsibility to safeguard the "priceless (not to mention irreplaceable) heritage" of the natural world? Is it, as some of the gloomier visionaries assert, too late already? Can we escape Paul Ehrlich's (*The Population Bomb*) hellish vision of a planet gradually suffocating under an ever-thickening blanket of humanity? Maybe, maybe not. The world is nothing if not a very uncertain and ever-changing place and none of these burning issues is exactly new. Concern for the fate of elephants dates back to Roman times. In a 19th century reminiscence, legendary hunter Frederick Courteney Selous wrote that, in 1874, he had found white rhinos "fairly plentiful" in the area of Botswana along the river Chobe. By 1879, however, he reported that they had completely vanished from the area. Selous expressed concern for their declining numbers, apparently unaware of anything inconsistent in the fact that he himself had "despatched" six during the period, including a mother and her baby. A century later, in the sort of seesaw scenario that has often characterized man's efforts to manage the natural world, the white rhino was brought back from extinction in Botswana when seventy-one animals were reintroduced to Chobe National Park and the Moremi Game Reserve between 1974 and 1981. That seed population was then supposed to increase naturally to about two-hundred and forty, but thanks to the poaching explosion, it didn't work out that way. By 1992 an aerial census found only seven white and zero black rhinos, after which an additional three whites were killed and the population once again dropped perilously close to the extinction level. Current estimates suggest that poaching has reduced the world population of black rhinos by an astounding 97% in the last thirty years. If ecotourism can provide a way out of this depressing spiral, now would certainly be a good time to find it out.

The preliminary signs seem hopeful. Tourism, according to a recent estimate by the World Travel and Tourism Council, will employ one of every nine workers worldwide in 1994, making it the world's largest industry. Within that industry, ecotourism is the fastest growing sector. On the other hand, such growth might quickly become a double-edged sword since it will necessarily require construction of the same sort of support facilities needed for old-fashioned tourism. As usual, the irony is inescapable. In the summer of 1991, the small Central American country of Belize hosted the first Caribbean Conference on Ecotourism, attended by three-hundred and fifty delegates. The conference took place at the Biltmore

Plaza, a hotel that had itself been built at the cost of destroying two distinct ecosystems, according to participant Dr. Erlet Cater, a lecturer in geography at Britain's University of Reading and a specialist in tourism to developing countries. Something similar happened on the rim of Tanzania's Ngorongoro Crater with the recent building of a new luxury hotel (a second one looms on the horizon)... to the accompaniment of a predictable chorus of criticism and lamentation from those who didn't think this was a great idea.

Apart from the sentiment that such places as Ngorongoro ought to be kept as pristine as possible because of their role as World Heritage sites, the arguments that can be mustered against this kind of development—presented by Raymond Bonner in his recent book, *At The Hand Of Man: Peril and Hope For Africa's Wildlife*—are numerous and persuasive. For one thing, Bonner points out, there's not enough water to support the 25,000 Maasai with their 250,000 cattle who already live in the area *and* all the additional tourists the owners are hoping will flock to these ultra-luxurious new gathering places. As before, the losers in such a competition are likely to be the Maasai and, eventually, the wildlife itself as the increased tourist traffic beats up and degrades the entire crater.

Dr. Cater, writing in the March 1992 issue of *Geographical Magazine*, states the conflict this way: "...there is a great danger that the sophisticated marketing and promotional strategies of travel and tour operators based in the more developed countries [MDCs] will lead to the false belief that ecotourism is a panacea for all tourism's ills. It is not even guaranteed to be ecologically sensitive, let alone sustainable as far as host populations, tourists and the environment itself are concerned. Yet to argue against ecotourism is to swim against the tide. In an increasingly environmentally conscious world the search for unspoiled nature will remain high on the tourist agenda. Ecotourism, despite its faults, is a lesser evil than uncontrolled mass tourism. Tour companies have eagerly jumped on this highly profitable bandwagon. At the same time they are able to promote a seemingly more conscientious image which may or may not go beyond shrewd marketing tactics. The inevitable outcome is that the main beneficiaries of ecotourism, as with tourism in general in the developing world, are tourism enterprises, all too often located in the MDCs. Unless the basic issues are addressed, ecotourism may well be regarded as a form of ecocolonialism."

It would be easy to come away from all these arguments and counter-arguments with the impression that the situation may well be hopeless—that we're damned if we do and damned if we don't. But isn't it better to be damned for *doing* something than for standing around helplessly wringing our hands in fretful despair? One of the most important things that can be done to relieve the problem of too many tourists in the parks is to open up more land to tourism. Richard Leakey had such plans in mind for Kenya, but it's not as easy as it sounds. An infrastructure has to be put in place—roads, lodges, security—and that will take time and money. The success of such a program will ultimately depend on the flow of tourist traffic and how much of the resulting economic benefit finds its way into the hands of the local populations. Unfortunately, the environmentalists—particularly the more radical members among them—seem increasingly to feel that *any* intrusion by man into the natural world is deplorable and ought to be prevented.

First introduced during the long agony of the Vietnam war, the seemingly deranged concept of destroying things in order to save them is now being applied to elephant populations in places where they are deemed, for one reason or another, to be too numerous. A remedy (which is not the same as a solution) has been found in an operation called "culling"—described with devastating and heartbreaking clarity by Cynthia Moss in her book, *Elephant Memories*: "A family is herded by helicopter or light aircraft toward waiting marksmen and all the members, except calves of about one to three years old, are shot and killed in a matter of a couple of minutes. The calves are captured for sale to zoos and safari parks. It would be a clean, quick operation except for the babies, who scream and mill about and climb over their dead relatives in an effort to find and stay with their mothers. This system of culling is thought to least disturb an elephant population and is used in preference to shooting a few animals from each family. No doubt it is less disturbing, but the elephants know very well what is going on and that knowledge appears to be communicated throughout the population."

How can such slaughter possibly be necessary when the elephant population throughout Africa has been variously reported to have declined by anywhere from twenty to eighty-six percent? Even if no one really knows how many elephants there are (which seems likely considering the difficulty of taking an accurate elephant census in an area of more than 250,000 square miles in over 90 national parks, never mind the rest of Africa), these dreary statistics have been relentlessly hammered into the public consciousness by the conservation community. Steven Andrews of Gaborone, Botswana, perhaps speaking for many, asks, "Who does man think he is to decree what and how many should be allowed to live? Before man encroached on their territory elephant were roaming the land that most towns and cities are built on today." Well, man thinks he is man of course and until lately, no other answer to Andrews' question was required.

Winston Churchill had one of these "who does man think he is" epiphanies during a 1908 safari when he shot a rhino but failed to kill it. The wounded animal, understandably aggravated, charged his attackers and was promptly greeted by a defensive and no doubt panicky barrage from everyone in the party. "Still the ponderous brute came on," Churchill wrote, "as if he were invulnerable, as if he were an engine, or some great steam barge impervious to bullets, insensible to pain or fear." At last, when he was only a few feet away, the rhino fell dead. In his subsequent account of the affair, recorded in *My African Journey*, Churchill wrote, "There is time to reflect with some detachment that, after all, we it is who have forced the conflict by an unprovoked assault with murderous intent upon a peaceful herbivore; that if there is such a thing as right and wrong between man and beast—and who shall say there is not?—right is plainly on his side."

Hunting, of course, is a natural activity far older than man. Until the dawn of agriculture and the domestication of livestock, the human species, like every other predator, depended on it for survival. It was hard, usually dangerous work. In our time, however, it has been more a sport than a necessity in much of the developed world, doubtless motivated to some degree by lingering traces of the age-old instinct that drove the hunter-gatherers of prehistory. Obviously, today's affluent Western hunters don't need to kill elephants or rhinos for food, and affluence is definitely required. In places where hunting is allowed, licenses to stalk such big game come at a steep price: $25,000 to $35,000 for a rhino in South Africa; $19,000 for a trophy bull elephant in Zimbabwe. Add to that the cost of the safari itself and hunters not uncommonly spend fifty or even one hundred thousand dollars for the privilege of launching unprovoked assaults with murderous intent on peaceful herbivores. Those with a taste for such things understand the power of this age-old killer instinct, but today's tide isn't running that way. More and more people seem to agree with Raymond Bonner who says, "I do not understand what it is that drives a man, or woman, to pick up a rifle and shoot an elephant, or a lion, or a leopard, or a kudu, for sport."

Not that Bonner is opposed to hunting. On a practical level, no serious conservationist could be because of the leading role hunters and hunting have long played in the effort to protect and conserve the world's wildlife. Even so, fear of the negative response from disapproving and ever more powerful animal rights groups and from the public at large prevents most conservation organizations from risking either membership loss or bad public relations by admitting that. From a purely economic point of view, however, hunters are probably a greater boon to the wildlife than ordinary tourists with their harmless cameras since they leave behind vastly greater quantities of money. And make no mistake, money is what it's all about. Bonner says that Costa Mlay, director of Tanzania's wildlife department, estimates that one hunter is worth a hundred non-hunting tourists.

The point appears to be reinforced by a 1990 report of Richard Leakey's on the Kenya Wildlife Service's five-year program, from which Bonner extracted this revealing quote: "Sport hunting appears to have the potential to generate more income for land owners from a given number of wild animals than do wildlife cropping or ranching, and possibly more than viewing tourism." However wacky and abhorrent it may seem to those who oppose hunting, the legal, carefully managed and controlled killing of wild animals can and probably will have to be regarded as a powerful tool in the struggle to conserve them.

In case you don't believe that money is the name of this game, Bonner points out that the cost of maintaining a park and protecting the animals against poaching, particularly elephants and rhinos, is generally accepted as between $200 and $400 per square kilometer. At that rate, Tanzania, with twenty-six percent of its land set aside as National Parks and Reserves (the U.S. has seven percent), would need $49 million to $98 million annually to do the job, but nothing even close to that amount is actually available. According to Clive Walker, a wildlife artist with credentials that include both founding and acting as director of the Endangered Wildlife Trust, "the available habitat for elephants in National Parks and protected areas can accommodate only 30% of the projected 625,000-strong elephant population [he admits that this projection is overly optimistic]. Over a total range of 500,000 square kilometers, African elephant protection will cost at present values something in the region of [$30 million] per annum if the job is to be done properly. Where will this money be raised? Perhaps the concerned West might undertake to share the burden? With the CITES edict [the ivory ban] continuing, the loss of revenue from necessary elephant culling and sale of products in southern Africa is seriously jeopardizing the present levels of protection unless alternative sources of funding can be found to replace it." There appears to be a slight discrepancy here. If Bonner's figures are accurate, that $30 million should actually be between $100 million and $200 million, but this isn't surprising. Hardly any two sources even agree as to the size of a national park, a fact that wouldn't appear on its face to be all that variable.

Of course, not all the wildlife lives in the National Parks (in Kenya, at least eighty percent lives outside them) and this compounds the protection problem—as if it needed compounding. Walker says the West, which he describes as "almost hysterical in its sudden concern for the elephant," has been widely misled into believing that the ivory trade was entirely to blame for the animals' decline. The truth, he maintains, "is that the states of central and east Africa should be ashamed at the contrast between the wholesale slaughter of their elephant populations and the good elephant management of the southern African states. Those countries which are fast losing their elephants will somehow have to be persuaded to accept responsibility themselves rather than blame oriental craftsmen who don't know the blunt from the sharp end of an elephant and don't care anyway."

Mark and Delia Owens, after years of watching poachers in Zambia's North Luangwa National Park turn the place into a virtual war zone in defiance of the ivory ban, might be skeptical of that rosy view of southern Africa's "good elephant management." Recording their harrowing adventures in *The Eye of the Elephant*, they attribute the slaughter that was going on in North Luangwa until very recently to the fact that those same southern African countries had refused to honor the ban and continued to traffic in illicit ivory. A black marketeer, who drunkenly misread the words "Conservation Project" on the side of Mark's truck as "Construction Project," tried to sell him some illegal items. He said that he survived "by selling to dealers in countries still trading" and that the poachers were "shooting elephants and burying ivories, waiting for America, Europe and Japan to refuse this foolish ban."

Can the Owens and Clive Walker both be right? Such apparent contradictions seem to demonstrate that there are as many versions of the "truth" as there are people to report it. Who you choose to believe depends on your own set of values, prejudices and beliefs and whether or not you have some agenda, which each of these observers obviously do.

The fabric of conservation strategy and philosophy has always been delicate and complex, subject to violent disruption and unraveling with sudden shifts of the political wind. As Peter Matthiessen observed in 1973, "...an outbreak of political instability might wreck the tourist industry that justifies the existence of the parks, thus removing the last barrier between the animals and a hungry populace. African schoolchildren are now taught to appreciate their wild animals and the land, but public attitudes may not change in time to spare the wildlife in the next decades, when the world must deal with the worst consequences of over-population and pollution. And a stubborn fight for animal preservation in disregard of people and their famine-haunted future would only be the culminating failure of the western civilization that, through its blind administration of vaccines and quinine, has upset the ecologies of a whole continent. Thus wildlife must be treated in terms of resource management in this new Africa which includes, besides gazelles, a growing horde of tattered humans who squat for days and weeks and months and years on end, in a seeming trance, awaiting hope."

Writing in 1993, Ronell Pienaar, a director and assistant editor of Botswana's *Wildlife Watch* magazine, said, "From the point of view of many ordinary rural Africans, the demands of the western world's conservation ideology have conflicted all too often with their legitimate needs. It therefore comes as no surprise to learn that wildlife conservation has failed across much of the continent and that such communities living in key conservation areas or alongside national parks or game reserves have come to view wildlife and tourism with, at best, indifference and, at worst, outright hostility."

How could this picture of the situation get any more dismal? Pienaar states the problem succinctly: "Whilst many retain the out-dated view of conservation as the preservation of our natural environment at any cost, the true challenge facing the present generation of conservationists is rather how to reconcile wildlife conservation priorities with the needs and aspirations of the people of Africa, and to link to conservation their economic, political and social development."

War, famine, poverty, illiteracy, overpopulation and pandemic AIDS (to name just a few of the continent's pervasive problems) sweep like endless grassfires through places like Somalia, Angola, Sudan and Ethiopia. But perhaps, underneath the headlines, it isn't quite the hopeless morass it seems. Africa may be, as TIME magazine writer Lance Morrow described it in a September 1992 cover story entitled *The Agony of Africa*, "the basket case of the planet, the 'Third World of the Third World...,'" but the story hardly ends there. Morrow himself later concedes that "in many ways the continent is headed in the right direction for the first time in centuries. Real changes for the better are occurring. Africa is evolving African solutions."

Enter CAMPFIRE (Communal Areas Management Programme For Indigenous Resources). In 1989, while the world's attention was focused on the elephant and the ivory ban, the residents of a local Zimbabwean community called Nyaminyami received from the government the right to exercise control over their wildlife. Of this watershed event Raymond Bonner said, "There were no front-page headlines, not even any news stories, but it was a critical step in a radical conservation program—one that will do more to save the elephant than the ban on ivory trading, and one that goes farther toward giving people the benefits of wildlife than anything being tried in Kenya or anywhere else on the continent." In Nyaminyami, as in much of rural Africa, wildlife constitutes the sole resource of any value. With the advent of CAMPFIRE, it became possible for the first time for the local citizens who live with the wildlife every day to reap not just some, but *all* of the rewards from its management. If there is indeed hope for Africa's wildlife, it probably lies in programs like CAMPFIRE, for without this kind of economic incentive for local populations, all the efforts of the conservation organizations may well be in vain.

In Nyaminyami, as elsewhere throughout Africa, a choice ultimately had to be made between wildlife and the cattle and agricultural activities that compete with it for value and space. In a convoluted way, this choice had long been linked to the infamous tsetse fly whose role as a carrier of the deadly *Trypanosoma* organism made it the scourge of both men and their cattle. The strain that causes encephalitis or "sleeping sickness" in man has largely been eradicated, but the cattle-killing variety remains active. Both originate in the blood of wild animals and are picked up by the tsetse flies that share the animals' woodland and bush habitat. Africans gained control of the flies by clearing the woods and bush around their villages on a limited scale. In that way, wildlife, cattle and man could coexist. But then the Europeans arrived and their plan for getting control of the situation was of the "swat the fly with a sledgehammer" persuasion: eradicate the wildlife, which they proceeded to do on a grand scale. With the flies under control, farmers could move in without worry. That meant more bad news for whatever remnants of wildlife there might be because, of course, the farmers didn't want wild animals competing with their livestock and destroying their crops. In Zimbabwe, the government still encourages all this because good farmland is scarce and it wants more cattle for export to the European market. Cotton may have been king in the antebellum American South, but in Africa cattle occupy that throne. As the South learned to its sorrow, however, one-crop economies can be very precarious.

How could the people of Nyaminyami and, eventually perhaps, other African communities, be persuaded to choose wildlife over cattle? Africans correctly perceive cattle as money in the bank. Therefore, somehow wildlife also had to be made into a bankable asset. That became the CAMPFIRE objective. The operative phrase for this is "sustainable utilization," big impressive words that cloak the underlying principle that wildlife, if it is to survive in a world it must increasingly share with an ever-expanding human population, will have to pay its own way and be harvested very much as its domestic counterparts are. How that harvest is carried out and by whom can take many directions, but the end purpose and result must remain the same; the conversion of wildlife into a renewable economic resource. We can lament this necessity, but we cannot escape it and save the wildlife at the same time.

Nature itself does not share our compunction about the process of extinction, a fact often overlooked or ignored in the environmentalists' arsenal of arguments. In the course of geologic time and the long evolution of life on earth, countless thousands of species have, like Omar Khayyam's ancient sultans, abode their destined hour and gone their way... all without our help. The dinosaurs, perhaps the most popular animals of all time because of their peculiar grip on the human imagination, ruled the earth for a stupefying 165 million years and then vanished completely. Science, for all its spectacular achievements, has yet to fully explain the mystery of that disappearance, but we can at least be absolutely certain that man was not to blame. In the heat of our recently awakened environmental and ecological consciousness, however, nature's routine wholesale elimination of species becomes awkward and inconvenient. If all the animals currently on the CITES Appendix I disappeared as the dinosaurs did, we would scratch our heads and say, "Well, it's just nature taking its usual mysterious and dispassionately brutal course." But when we are the direct cause of such disappearances, the whole picture suddenly changes. As the late cartoonist Walt Kelly once put it, "We have met the enemy and he is us."

We tend to see ourselves, not as an integral part of nature, but as spectators and manipulators of the drama. Even though the periodic unleashing of nature's immense powers can easily destroy us and all our works without regard for our intelligence and technology, we and our activities have clearly been responsible for propelling various species into oblivion. Because these activities continue to threaten still more species with the same fate, environmentalists have determined (perhaps correctly) that we are responsible for the future of the planet and all its inhabitants. After taking a more or less heedless view of this question of responsibility for centuries, the pendulum has swung in the opposite direction. We now appear to be at the other end of the arc. Somehow, if we are in fact to save something of the natural world for future generations to know and enjoy, we will have to get closer to the balance point.

CAMPFIRE offers one effective way to do exactly that. True, the animal rights people will claim that we have no moral or ethical right to make the kind of life-and-death decisions for wildlife that such management techniques as culling represent. That may well be so, but the truth is that we have no other realistic option unless, of course, we want to start managing our own population that way. If all these problems result from an uncontrolled explosion in human numbers, should we solve them by culling people rather than elephants? If Africa has 700 million people and only 600 thousand elephants, which is more expendable? In today's climate, it is easy for those who are far removed from the reality of the problem to ask such questions and to wonder if human rights, needs and desires do legitimately take precedence over those of every other creature. But would anyone seriously suggest that the solution lies in culling people, even though we have frequently resorted to exactly that strategy for achieving various objectives ("ethnic cleansing" in Bosnia being but the most recent deplorable example)? Not likely. The preservation of some other species has

31

never been among the ends we've used to justify that particular means. Nevertheless, a recent development in Zimbabwe seems encouraging. With help from the U.S. Fish and Wildlife Service and a British organization called Care for the Wild, whole elephant families—some 600 individuals between August and December 1993—have been tranquilized and relocated rather than culled.

For their part, the elephants would scarcely mourn our passing. After all, they and their ancestors were here before we came and they would doubtless view the world as a better, less dangerous place without us. Imagine how we would respond if a gang of elephants launched a culling campaign to control the destructive hordes of humans invading their habitat, devastating their forage areas, and killing, not just a few, but tens of thousands of their relatives and neighbors. Only man is capable of such concepts and actions, of course. The elephants are, as far as we can tell, indifferent to our fate. It is beyond their power to be responsible for us, but it is not beyond our power to be responsible for them. CAMPFIRE and programs like it could take on that responsibility in the most effective and perhaps even the most humane possible way.

So far it has been a success, at least in Nyaminyami. Once we get away from the common mistake of applying inappropriate Western ideologies and concepts to Third World realities, it's easy to see why. Raymond Bonner, who visited Nyaminyami and even went along (with some trepidation) on an impala cull, explains that Nyaminyami "earned enough from hunting in 1989 to pay the costs of running its own conservation program. With the money, the district hired twelve game rangers, provided them with uniforms, rifles, shovels, tents and rations, and paid them the equivalent of $100 a month. It was one of the best-paid, best-equipped ranger units in Africa." It stands to reason. Only a fool would let some poacher trespass on his land to kill and steal animals that might be worth as much as $20,000 apiece. Bonner quotes Simon Metcalfe, who has worked with CAMPFIRE in Nyaminyami from the beginning: "From being one of the poorest areas in Zimbabwe, I predict that within a decade it could be one of the wealthiest." Metcalfe "calculated that by the mid-1990s, Nyaminyami will be earning $500,000 a year from wildlife, which is about $500,000 more than the district has now [in 1990] from all sources, except foreign aid."

And what animal brings in the most money? The elephant of course, because it's the major lure for hunters out to bag big game trophies. The current fee of $19,000 for a trophy bull is more than five times what it was in 1989, so the chances are that Metcalfe's prediction will prove correct. Add to that the incidental benefits of meat, skins and other by-products, and the even more exciting possibility of remunerative joint ventures with tourist operations, and you have the makings of a wildlife cornucopia. Bonner says, "In the past, before CAMPFIRE came along, only a small portion of the income generated by wildlife in Zimbabwe was returned to the districts where the wildlife was found; and even then the return was indirect in the form of, say, a school or a health clinic or the grading of a road. This is the pattern throughout Africa: wildlife proceeds generally go into the national treasury and are then more likely to be used for paving a road in a wealthy section of the capital than for extending electricity to a rural area."

Mark and Delia Owens support the sustainable utilization concept, although perhaps not the hunting aspect of it. After several agonizing and perilous years of what seemed like a hopeless struggle, they finally prevailed in their war against the poachers of Zambia's North Luangwa National Park through sheer guts and determination. In 1992, thanks at least in part to their campaign, the new government announced that Zambia would rejoin and fully support the ivory ban. At the close of their book, *The Eye of the Elephant*, they summed up their view of what the future might hold: "Until substantial benefits can be realized from tourism and other wildlife related industries, the North Luangwa Conservation Project must continue to find ways of fostering an economic bond between the park's animal communities and nearby villages, which might otherwise destroy the wildlife. The short-term advantages to the villagers eventually must be replaced by sustainable benefits that come directly from the park. Tourism may be the answer, but it must be designed so that it does not disrupt the ecosystem. Everything is ready... all that remains is for tourists to come. Each person who comes and walks in the real Africa helps save elephants by making living wild animals valuable to the local people."

Far from Nyaminyami and North Luangwa, in 1993 the residents of Papua New Guinea set aside one thousand square miles of some of the last undisturbed rainforest in the world as a wildlife preserve—an act that could set a new tone for international conservation efforts. The New York Zoological Society and the Wildlife Conservation Society worked with members of twenty different clans for several years to make this a reality. Such an approach departs radically from the past practice of appealing strictly to national governments to establish such preserves. "The indigenous peoples' land rights are very important. You can't just build a fence and push people out. That's the old-fashioned view," said a representative of the South Pacific Program at the World Wide Fund for Nature (formerly the World Wildlife Fund). Offers from loggers and developers were countered by establishing research centers in the area, sending in the Peace Corps and promoting ecotourism. The Wildlife Conservation Society is pursuing similar ventures in Zaire, Congo, Venezuela and Panama.

By and large, the big conservation organizations also support this principle of sustainable utilization, but they fear reprisal for that support from animal rights militants. Their fear is hardly groundless since they have, indeed, been publicly vilified for it. Their lack of candor on the issue may appear to suggest, as Bonner claims, that they lack the courage of their convictions, but on the other hand the power of today's activists, who may or may not behave in a responsible or even truthful way, can be formidable and costly. The damage to a conservation organization's image and reputation, once done, may be heavy and irreversible. Perhaps their wariness is, if not the better part of valor, at least the better part of realism.

The conservation organizations have also been criticized for their way of playing this tricky political game. As former game ranger Ian Parker says in his book, *Ivory Crisis*, "The evidence is both glaring and irrefutable: conservation is a field which has become characterized by lies, half-truths and outright distortion. Central to the evolution of this sad state of affairs is a belief that the public only reacts and donates funds in response to sensation and crisis. The media support this view because sensation sells copy and film footage." The charge has validity. Donate money to one of these organizations and you will soon be subjected to a steady bombardment of "urgent" appeals for more money to help stave off the imminent destruction of some species or habitat. All these emergencies may be real enough, but such overkill tends to erode their credibility and impact.

With our ever-greater understanding of animal behavior, achieved through the efforts of such renowned field biologists as Niko Tinbergen, George Schaller, Jane Goodall, Dian Fossey, and Cynthia Moss, we have gradually come around to seeing that we are not the only sentient beings with social and family structures or the ability to have emotional responses to pain, suffering and the joys of life. Perhaps Walt Disney launched us on the road to that awareness in the early 1940s when he made such hugely popular and enduring animated films as *Bambi* and *Dumbo*. Those sentimental films made their animal stars not only endearing, but *just like us*. It was anthropomorphism at its most blatant, but then maybe animals really *are* just like us in many ways. Other films on animal themes, like 1963's *Mondo Cane*, shocked Western sensibilities by revealing that, in some parts of the world, man's best friend is a routine entrée on the menu along with a lot of other, more exotic creatures from monkeys to snakes.

With this expansion of understanding through observation came a change in our attitude toward the role of animals and our relationship to them. As Henry Beston put it in *The Outermost House*, "We need another and a wiser and perhaps a more mystical concept of animals. Remote from universal nature, and living by complicated artifice, man in civilization surveys the creature through the glass of his knowledge and sees thereby a feather magnified and the whole image in distortion. We patronize them for their incompleteness, for their tragic fate of having taken form so far below ourselves. And therein we err, and greatly err. For the animal shall not be measured by man. In a world older and more complete than ours, they move finished and complete, gifted with extensions of the senses we have lost or never attained, living by voices we shall never hear. They are not brethren, they are not underlings; they are other nations, caught with ourselves in the net of life and time, fellow prisoners of the splendour and travail of the earth."

It's easy to become cynical about all this. Greed and corruption follow money and power. Introduce native populations like the Maasai to the pernicious pitfalls of a money-driven economy and you risk introducing them to the root of all evil. What will happen to their cultures? Will they lie, cheat, steal and, worse, kill for a bigger share of the profit—just as we do? If hunting is reopened in Kenya, will neighboring countries follow suit? And if they do, will that be followed by discount wars that turn the forests and plains blue with gunsmoke? Are men anywhere likely to have better luck controlling hunting abuses than they have controlling drugs and crime? Under every rock lurks a nest of such hostile scorpions, stingers at the ready. Sustainable utilization and ecotourism may not be perfect solutions and no doubt the abuses that abound in more "advanced" societies will also occur in Africa, but they could hardly be worse than those of the past or those that are occuring now. In any case, what choice do we have?

In the 1950s, the on-going confrontation between loggers and spotted owls in the Pacific Northwest would have been unimaginable. In the 1990s, the comic strip *Calvin and Hobbes* shows us a flying saucer busily engaged in vacuuming away all of earth's oxygen, a valuable commodity on their home world. The alien crew informs the asphyxiating humans below, "We're sorry, but we prefer your extinction to the loss of our jobs." On the surface at least, this seems not only witty, but highly relevant. Just such a face-off appears to be going on all over the globe as we approach the year 2000. Who will win? The message of sustainable utilization is, we can all win, but not without a price. Whatever the irony, history and nature have always taught us that some must die so that others might live. Regrettable as that may be, it remains an inescapable reality if we are to preserve not only our wilderness and wildlife heritage, but ourselves.

ON SAFARI

41

Acacia trees silhouetted against a sunset may be Africa's most recognizable landscape, but the continent's scenery provides riches of every imaginable variety from farmland near Nairobi, to South Africa's Blyde River Canyon, to the red earth of the Namib desert.

45

From Kenya to the Cape of Good Hope, the faces of Africa's people both reflect and conceal the painful and complex choices facing the continent. Competition between man and wildlife for living space intensifies yearly. Ironically, each needs the other for survival. Only when that link is fully recognized will the future of the wildlife be assured.

Green tea rolls across the Kenyan hills at Mrs. Mitchell's Klambethu Tea Farm, about an hour's drive from Nairobi. Mrs. Mitchell was born here in 1909. Today, when visitors come, she prepares a lavish buffet lunch and recounts her family history and the story of tea with impressive energy and wit. Tea and coffee (the latter once grown by Isak Dinesen on her farm not far away) make up a major part of Kenya's exportable crops.

Together with Switzerland's Matterhorn and Japan's Mt. Fuji, Tanzania's Mt. Kilimanjaro stands as one of the world's most dramatically recognizable landmarks and the highest mountain on the African continent. At 19,340 feet, it utterly dominates the horizon in Kenya's Amboseli National Park and provides a favorite backdrop for photographers—when it chooses to appear from behind the clouds that often shroud it. Its association with Amboseli has led many visitors to conclude that it belongs to Kenya, a source of irritation to Tanzanians. Surprisingly, its snowy flanks and frigid summit support a rich variety of wildlife, including a subspecies of hyrax specifically adapted to its harsh environment. The largest pair of elephant tusks ever recorded weighed some 440 pounds and belonged to an old bull killed on its slopes in 1898. Today, Amboseli hosts more than 700 elephants which, with Kilimanjaro, constitute the park's main attractions. Within its boundaries, Cynthia Moss has carried out groundbreaking research on elephants that has revealed how closely their lives resemble our own.

In Africa, as everywhere, the contest between man and wildlife revolves around land. Wildebeest darken the Serengeti Plains as buffalo once darkened the American prairie little more than a century ago. We have learned much since then. As the end of the twentieth century approaches, we know we must find a way to live and let live or lose much of what remains of the wild world forever.

Comics of the antelope family, wildebeest (also known as white-bearded gnu, blue wildebeest and brindled gnu) have buffalo-like heads attached to cattle-sized bodies. Running about on the plains, their antic jiggings and leapings seem to suggest very playful natures. It is well that they are so prolific because the mortality rate from a wide variety of hazards is extremely high, sometimes as much as 50 percent. Their annual mass migrations back and forth across the Serengeti (far right inset) have made them among the best known of Africa's antelopes. In the evening's dusty light at Amboseli (bottom), their resonant blartings and honkings can be heard at great distances. The lone animal at Etosha National Park in Namibia (center inset) risks attack by predators. Their survival depends on the protection of numbers.

Ethereal greater and lesser flamingoes gathering by the thousands on Lake Magadi in Tanzania's Ngorongoro Crater and Kenya's Lake Nakuru, wear their peculiar smiles upside down. Each has a highly specialized bill adapted for straining and processing a totally different diet. Greater flamingoes, larger and paler in color, thrive on insect larvae, crustaceans and seeds while their deep pink cousins rely on diatoms and fine blue-green algae. Because of these extraordinary adaptations, they can forage together in huge concentrations without competing for food. They build cone-shaped nests of mud in which they usually incubate a single egg for a month. Migratory movements most often occur at night to provide greater protection from predators.

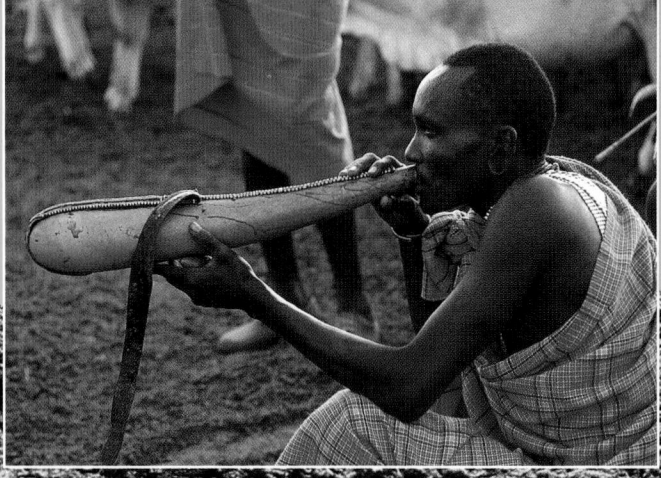

56

The Maasai culture revolves around cattle which give them milk (above left), blood to mix it with for a potent and nutritious drink (left center and bottom), dung to blend with mud and straw for building (detail strip), as well as wealth and social standing in the community (bottom right). Each animal wears its owner's brand (top right) and some even sleep in the master's house at night (far right inset). In the Maasai world view, **all** cattle rightfully belong to them. Taking cattle from other ranchers isn't rustling—it's merely fulfilling God's will.

"When the cows come home…"

*Man's world of the Maasai: as male youths mature, they become **Ilmoran** or warriors (top and lower middle) and go to live in special kraals called manyattas. **Ilmoran** must, among other ritual things, spear a lion to prove courage although the practice has been forbidden by the government. During this time in their lives, they accumulate cattle (often by staging raids on other Maasai kraals), protect the home kraal and perform numerous other tasks. Elegant and dignified, they wear beaded jewelry made for them by their girlfriends. When they become elders, they marry—usually more than once—and have children. Old age is not a fearful time for the Maasai, but one of serenity in which their wisdom and experience are valued and admired by the community. Ironically, the Maasai's traditional culture may vanish with the wildlife and for the same reason: loss of their land.*

60

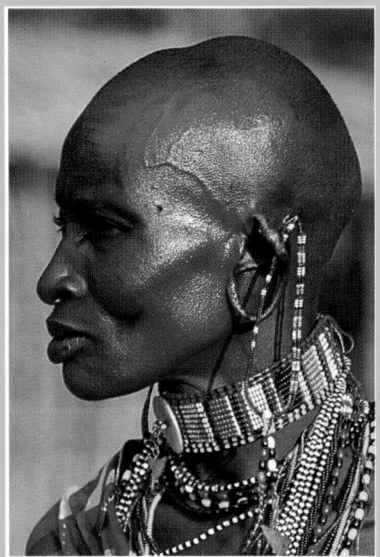

Maasai women mate for life, but share their husbands with numerous other wives. Wives may have other lovers and even have children by them, but the children must remain with the husband. The Maasai, who view divorce as nearly unthinkable and build their society on strong family unity, have great difficulty understanding western concepts of marriage.

KILLERS AND KINGS

*The big cats—lions, tigers,
leopards, jaguars, cougars and
cheetahs—have always held a
particular fascination for man,
perhaps because we admire their
grace and fear their predatory
power. Usually, we see lions—the
so-called king of beasts—snoozing
in the sun and conclude that they
lead idyllic lives of fearless ease.
Nothing could be farther from the
truth. Hunting is a laborious, high
stakes, hit or miss business. In times
of scarcity or drought, the margin
of survival becomes very narrow.
These lions and cheetahs, with
their catches of impala, warthog
and zebra, have been successful,
but tomorrow may be a different
story. Even though adults may
be at the top of their food chain,
they have enemies besides man
and cubs don't always survive
to join the hunt. As Shakespeare
observed, "Uneasy lies the head
that wears a crown."*

THE ENDLESS CYCLE OF LIFE AND DEATH

Lion cubs learn many of life's lessons in
play. Romping on a termite mound, they
develop physical agility and sharpen their
reflexes—both mandatory for successful
hunting. Occasionally, a mother lion will
leave her cubs on a termite mound, where
they may be somewhat protected from
prowling leopards and hyenas, while she
goes off in search of dinner. But they don't
always stay put and casualties can be
high. A pride followed by Frans Lanting in
Okavango had not succeeded in raising
one cub to maturity in ten years.

Thomson's gazelles have a host of enemies from cheetahs to eagles and pythons. Small, swift and graceful, their ability to reproduce every six months helps insulate the species against relentless predation. Males vie with each other for harems by butting heads and marking their territories in several ways, including smearing plants with secretions from preorbital glands. Large numbers of Thomson's gazelles often roam the plains in company with groups of Grant's gazelle (distinguished from Thomson's by their larger size and less conspicuous black side markings), wildebeest and zebra.

Aerialists among the antelope, graceful impala, when alarmed, seem to defy gravity by leaping away into the bush in thirty-five foot bounds at speeds approaching forty miles per hour. A female (only the males have horns) easily vaults across a stream in Samburu National Park (top left). An alert male stands guard over his harem in the Zambezi River valley (center left) and two males in the Masai Mara (bottom left) duel for possession of a female. One of the larger antelopes, impala graze the savannas in groups of anywhere from six to two hundred or more.

Family outing at the old swimming hole—an Amboseli group gathers at a spring to drink, cool off and play.

THE AMAZING TRUNK

Among the most versatile pieces of anatomy in all of nature, an elephant's trunk serves it nearly as well as our hands serve us. Its uses include sniffing the air for signs of danger and trumpeting warnings if any are detected, picking grass, shepherding the young, drinking, administering parasite-discouraging dust baths, and obtaining hard-to-reach delicacies. It remains in almost constant motion, snuffling the ground in search of tidbits and mineral salts, greeting and playing with friends, plucking leaves and fruit from trees, scratching, hosing water or dust and exploring the inquisitive owner's every curiosity as it ambles through the day. Strong enough to lift a good-sized tree, it is also sensitive and delicate enough to pick up a pebble—or take a single peanut from your hand at the zoo.

Elephants' gargantuan appetites (they will consume as much as three-hundred pounds of food in a single day) lead to widespread devastation of the landscape—especially trees—wherever they congregate in any numbers. Much of Amboseli, for example, now resembles a bomb-blasted war zone thanks to the foraging of its elephants. This characteristic, which often leads to crop-raiding, brings elephants into conflict with man, increasing the pressure that has reduced their numbers and threatens their survival.

Samburu National Park boasts several distinctive animals not found elsewhere: Grevy's zebra (top inset); the graceful gerenuk (center inset), also called the giraffe-necked antelope or Waller's gazelle and the only one of the antelopes to feed in this upright manner; and the reticulated giraffe (bottom inset). The Kirk's dik-dik (second from top inset), stands only thirteen to seventeen inches high. Only the Pygmy or Royal antelope of West Africa is smaller. The fringe-eared oryx (second from bottom inset) is one of seven oryx subspecies that once roamed all of Africa. They have been exterminated over two-thirds of their former range by man.

Elongated faces, prominent canine teeth and four-footed locomotion gave baboons the nickname "dog monkey." Authorities put the number of subspecies at anywhere from seven to thirty, but taxonomic disputes aside, all look much alike apart from slight variations in color and other minor differences. Intelligent, highly sociable and well-organized, they live in large packs, foraging by day and taking refuge from marauding predators—chiefly leopards— in trees or rocks at night. They have been described as brutal and ferocious, which no doubt they can be when the occasion demands, but they are also playful and gregarious. They will eat almost anything and consume large numbers of insects, a beneficial habit somewhat diminished by crop-raiding and egg-stealing. Many show great curiosity and little fear of man.

THE DOG MONKEYS

The young olive baboon (near right) and black-faced vervet monkey (far right, upper and middle) are the most commonly seen primates on a typical safari. The brazen vervets frequent areas around lodges and camps, ever vigilant for a handout or an opportunity to steal some goodies. Visitors regard this African equivalent of the squirrel as cute, but they can also be aggressive and belligerent, particularly when carrying babies. Armed with fierce teeth, they should be treated with caution and respect. The blue monkey (bottom right), on the other hand, rarely strays from the forest.

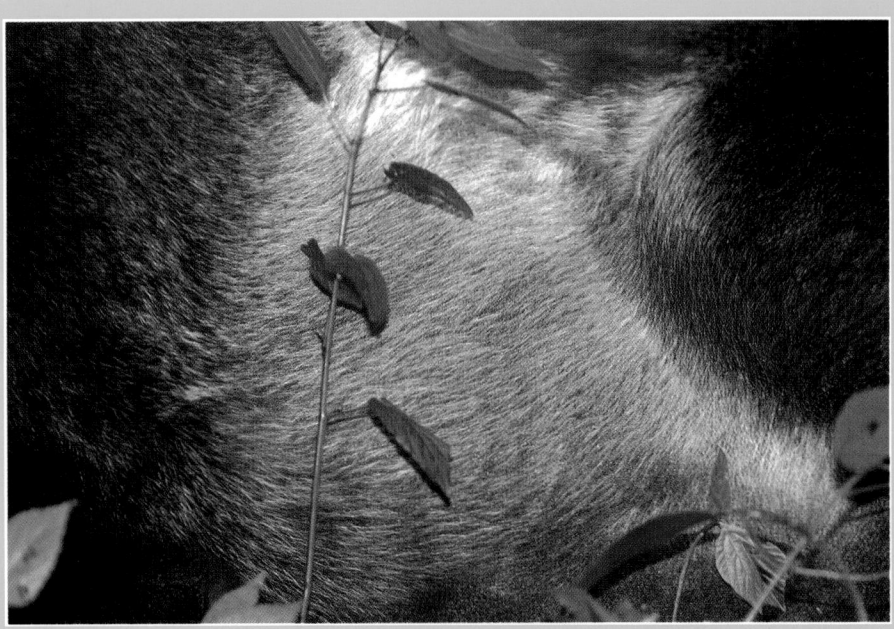

"...the next two decades are estimated to see the extinction of twenty species of animals. Human beings must decide now whether or not the mountain gorilla will become one of them, a species discovered and extinct within the same century. The gorillas' destiny lies in the hands of those who share their communal inheritance, the land of Africa, the home of the mountain gorilla."

Dian Fossey
Gorillas In The Mist

"THE THINKER"

More than any other animal except perhaps the chimpanzee, gorillas strike strong responsive chords in most humans. Sadly, they now hover precariously on the edge of extinction. Their once fearsome reputation, immensely and unfairly augmented by films like **King Kong**, has been largely dispelled by the efforts of the late Dian Fossey who went to study and live among them in 1966. Only minor differences of size, color and density of coat distinguish mountain from lowland gorillas. Full-grown males of either species can weigh up to 450 pounds and stand six feet tall. For all their size and strength they, like the elephants, are sensitive and gentle creatures with strong family structures. This family lives in Zaire's Kahuzi-Biega National Park and has become accustomed to human visitors. Even when no tourists come, the rangers visit the gorillas every day to maintain their familiarity with people.

Ugly by human standards, warthogs possess faces that only a mother could love, but their comic qualities make them almost lovable in spite of this affliction. Shuffling along on their knees while rooting for food with their formidable tusks, or trotting briskly about the savanna in family groups usually with tasseled tails sticking straight up, the response they most often evoke is laughter. Like all members of the swine family, however, they can be fierce and aggressive when the need arises. Their name derives from the peculiar facial excrescences prominently displayed on the individual at left.

A yellow-billed hornbill appears grumpy, but in fact its normal look suggests irritation. The bill consists of a horny covering over a bony mesh filled with air chambers, making it less heavy than it looks. With it, the male seals his mate up in a hollow tree with mud, then feeds her through a tiny hole while she lays and hatches her eggs. The ground hornbill (above) seldom flies because of its great size — three and a half feet from beak to tail. It usually walks around in pairs or family groups. No musician, it grunts like a lion.

*White animals with black stripes, or black animals with white stripes? Dealer's choice. The ancient Romans called them **hippotigris** (horse-tiger) and used them in their circuses. Three varieties—the mountain (not pictured), Grevy's (bottom left and right) and two color variants of the Burchell's (upper and center left)— survive today. A fourth, the quagga, became extinct more than a century ago. The Grevy's, largest of the zebras, can be distinguished by its large ears and narrower pattern of stripes.*

Wings Over Africa

Flying safaris, like Ker & Downey's **Wings Over Tanzania**, eliminate grueling hours of bone-jarring, dust-eating travel over Africa's rustic roads. The hours normally spent driving can be devoted to game drives and walks instead, a major advantage for the traveler with limited time and a strong interest in wildlife. Only from the air can the full spectacle of the annual migration of millions of wildebeest and zebra across the Serengeti be appreciated. At night, visitors gather around a fire at their tented camp to relive the day's adventures. Comfortable without being luxurious, the camps are permanent and usually remote. An efficient staff attends to everything, including laundry, while guests roam the park.

Balloonists fly at dawn from Governors' Camp in the Masai Mara. After an hour or two of floating over the savanna, they descend for a traditional champagne breakfast. Guests receive certificates signed by the pilot commemorating their flight.

Tip of the iceberg, the alert head of this hippopotamus may be attached, beneath the burnished water, to as much as 7,000 additional pounds of river horse. Living in large groups wherever deep pools can be found (following pages), they lead mostly aquatic lives, emerging at night to graze. Their heroic yawns, probably the most awesome in all of nature, denote aggression rather than fatigue. Males' lower canines may reach a length of twelve to fifteen inches or more and make formidable weapons. Jousting over territory, males chase each other with surprising agility and speed, making a great deal of water-churning racket. Babies, well-tended by their mothers, often clamber about on indulgent adults' backs.

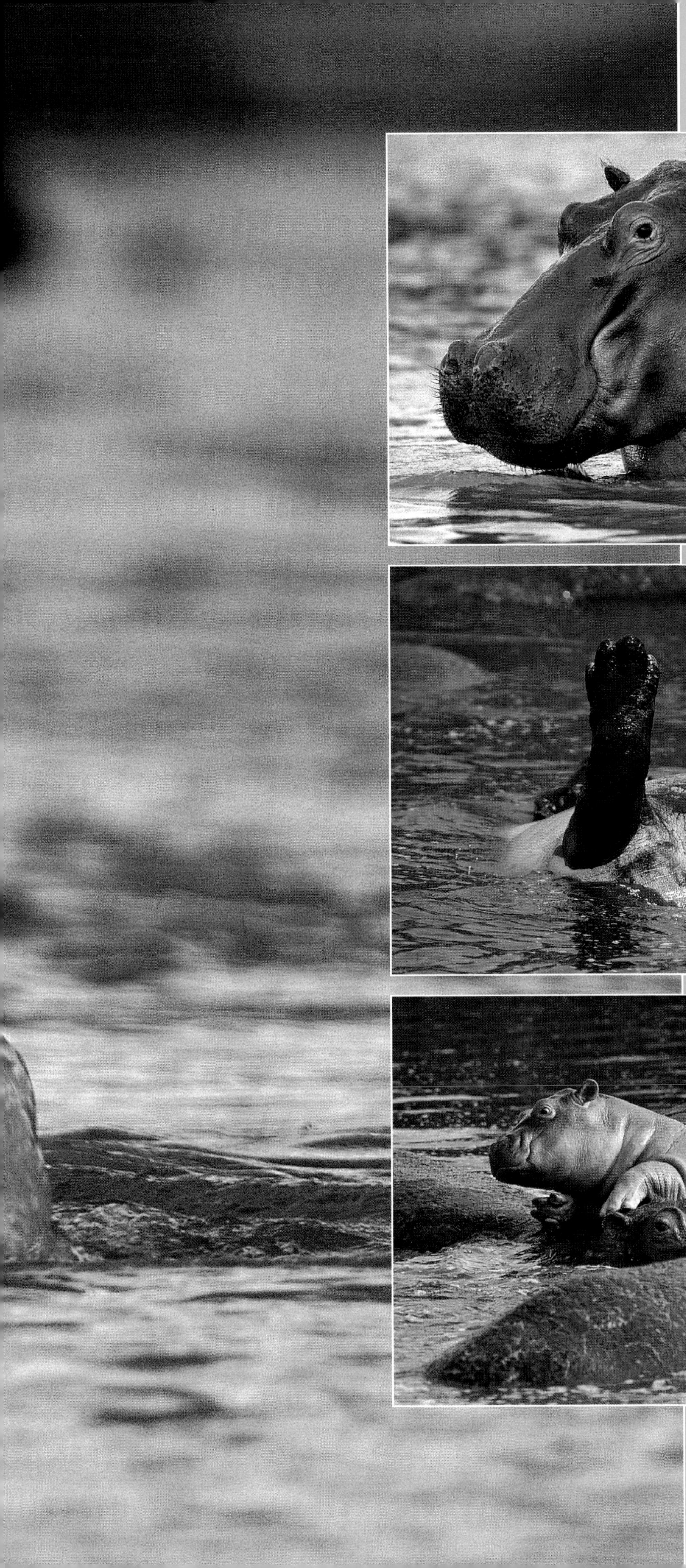

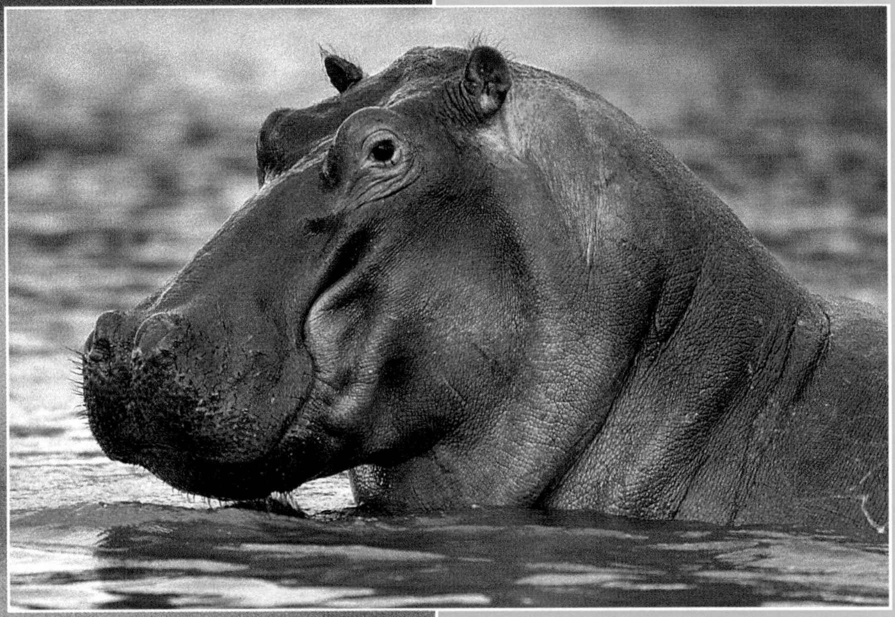

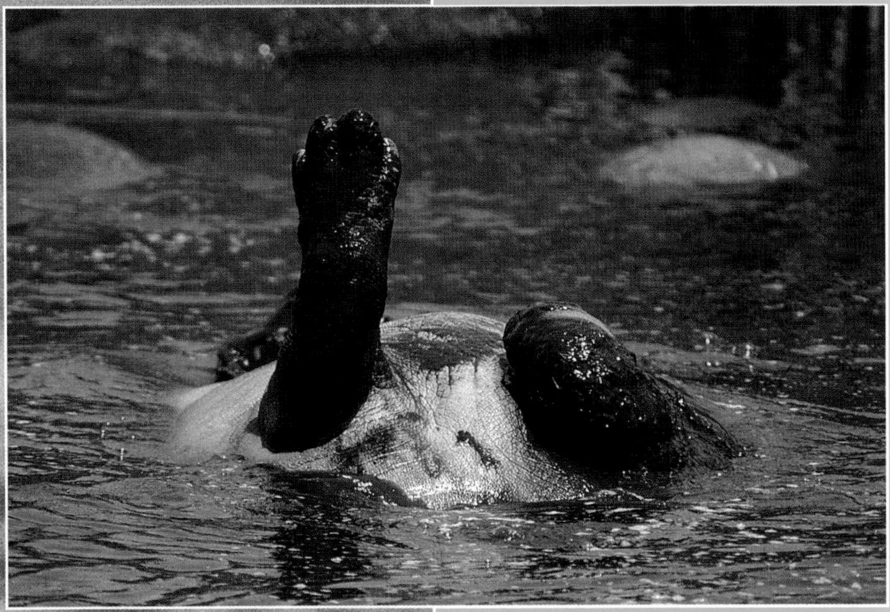

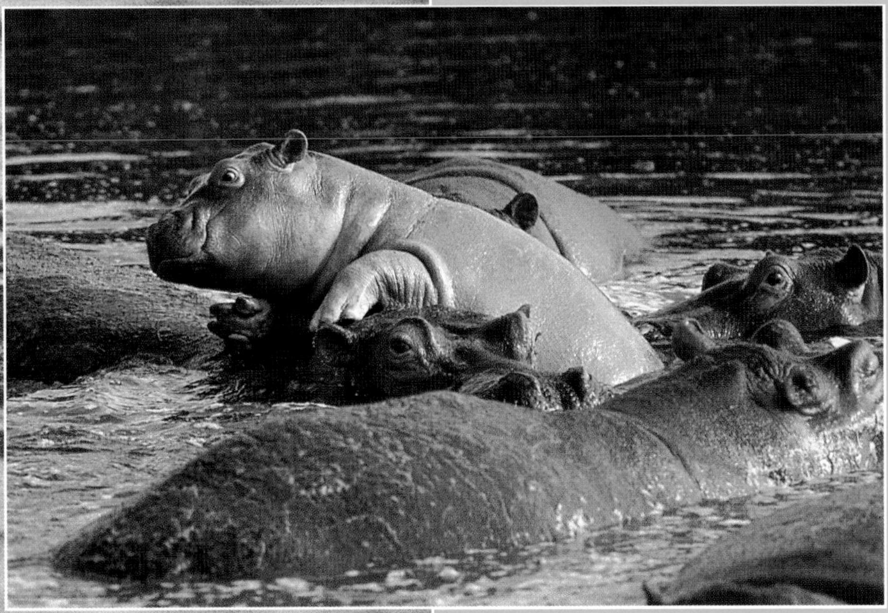

The Office Water Cooler

In what seems to be a universal tradition, park staffers gather around the water cooler. For some, like the giraffe, the business of drinking can be hazardous. Getting their heads down to the water leaves them in an awkward and vulnerable position. Elephants, on the other hand, don't even have to bend over as they suck up a few gallons at a time with their trunks. For others, like the zebra, wildebeest, impala and waterbuck, strength and security come from numbers. Knowing the risks, most animals become more wary than usual around waterholes, especially in times of drought. The outward appearance of a peaceable kingdom belies the fact that survival for most of Africa's wildlife requires ceaseless vigilance.

Kicking up clouds of characteristic dry season dust, a herd of wildebeest marches across the floor of Ngorongoro Crater, the world's largest unbroken, unflooded caldera.

Horns Of A Dilemma

A last lingering remnant of the giant mammals that once roamed the earth, Africa's rhinos may become extinct in the wild by the end of the century because of the value men have placed on their horns. Like human hair, the horns are composed entirely of keratin and have the same medicinal value—none. Their virtue as material for dagger handles may be arguable, but is it a moral act to consign a species as wondrous as the rhino to oblivion only to arouse our sex drives and decorate a few knives? The black rhino, with its distinctive prehensile upper lip, has been reduced by poaching from thousands to mere hundreds in the past two decades. If the traffic in horn continues, their survival seems unlikely.

A mother white rhino and her hefty baby have only about 3,032 wild relatives left in the world, according to the San Diego Zoo's Wild Animal Park where a successful breeding program for the species has been underway for years. Of that number, 3,000 live in South Africa where it is still possible to obtain a license to kill surplus bulls for a fee of between twenty-five and thirty-five thousand dollars. Their name comes from the Dutch word for wide rather than their color and refers to their square upper lips which distinguish them from black rhinos.

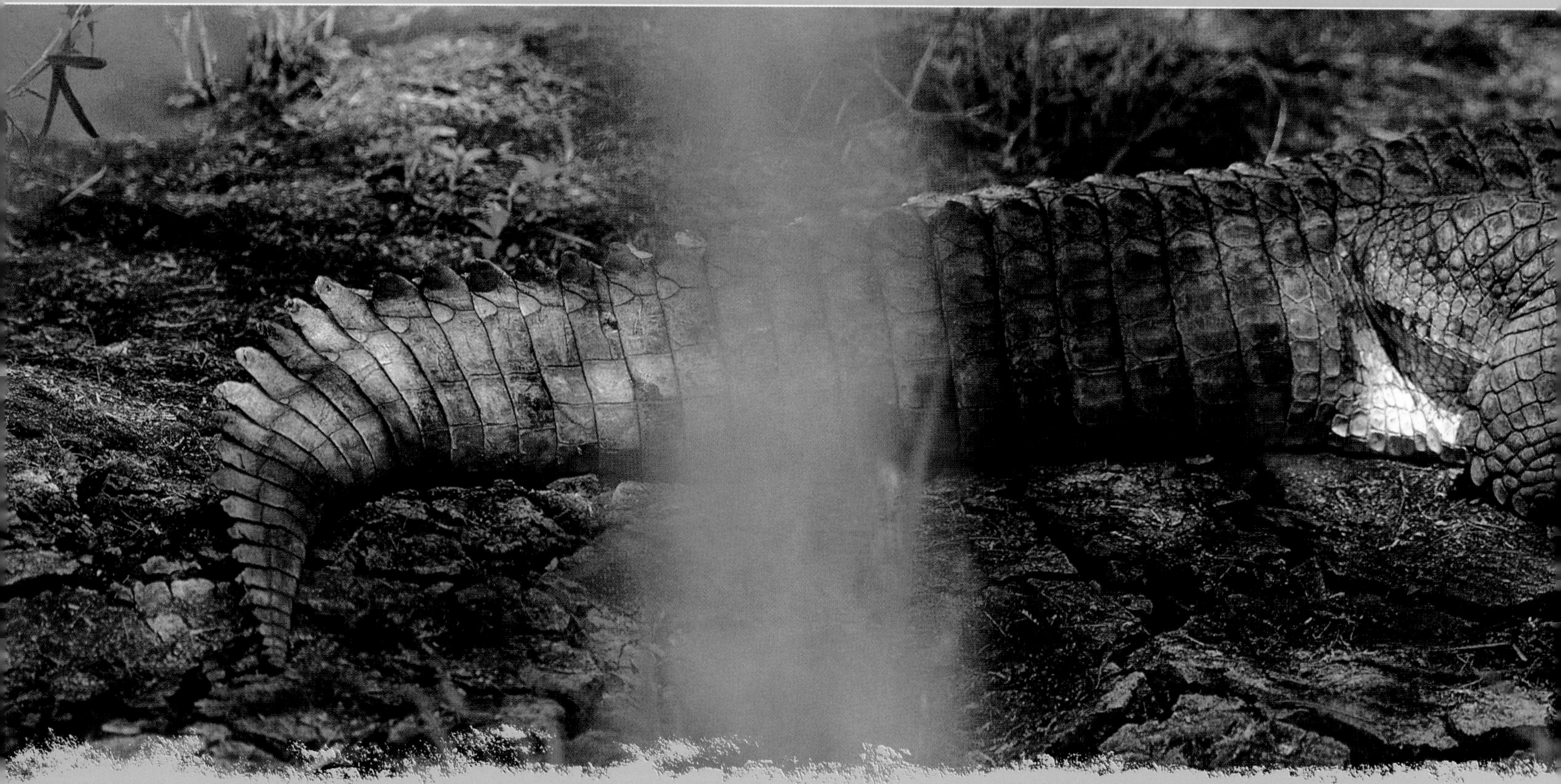

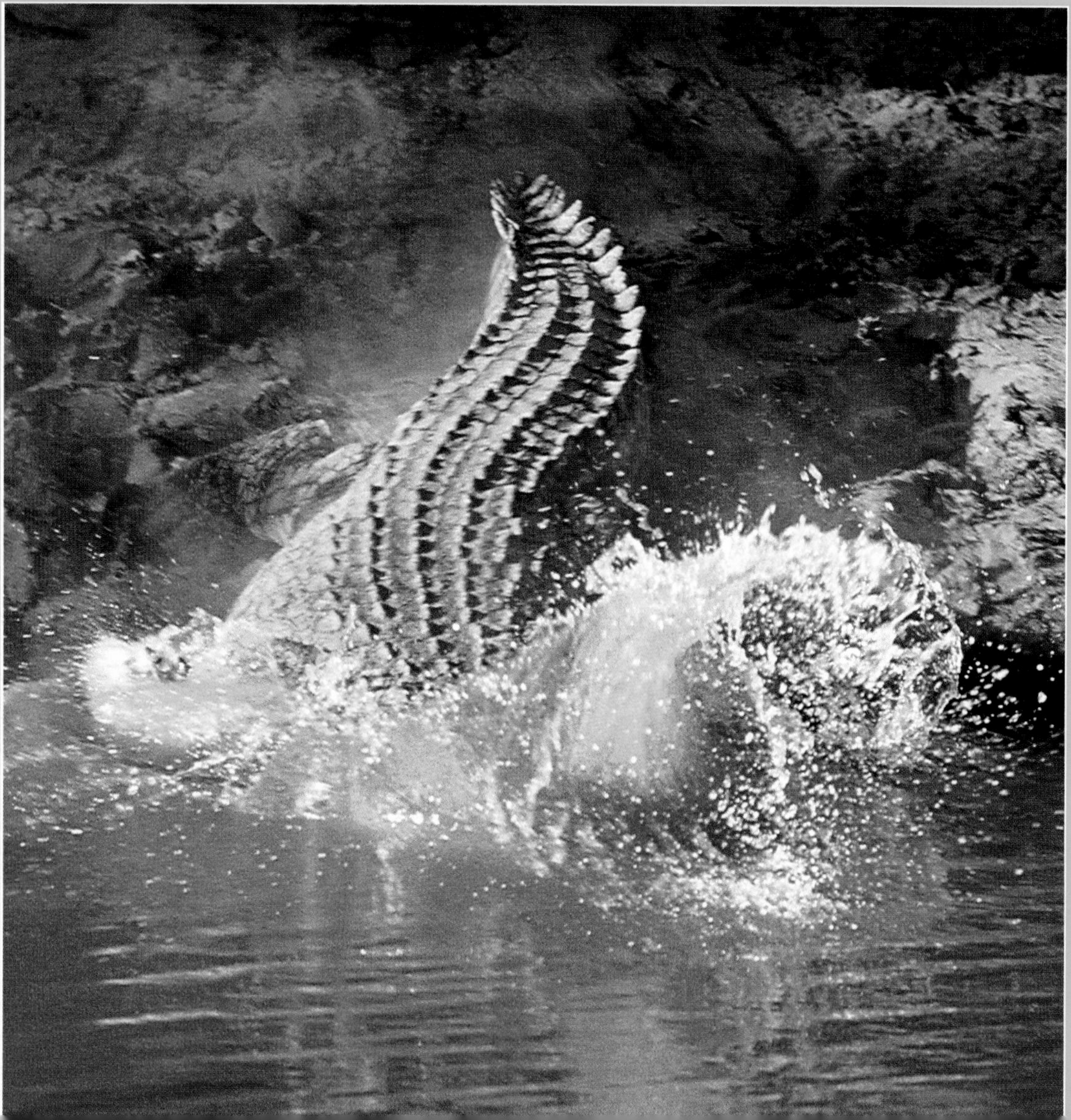

*Man's fear of the living animal and fondness
for the look of its hide in various leather
accessories has caused a drastic reduction
in the Nile crocodile population over much
of its former range. Up to fifteen feet long
and equipped with enormously powerful jaws
as well as surprising speed and agility, the
crocodile is a stealthy stalker. Cruising unseen
below the water's surface or lurking at its edge,
it literally explodes into action to seize unwary
prey and drag it below to drown. With teeth
designed to hold rather than cut, it entangles a
catch too large to swallow whole in underwater
growth or submerged tree branches and leaves
it to soften. It then tears off chunks by biting
and rolling. Females deposit tidy layers of up
to ninety five three-inch eggs in a hollowed-out
nest and cover them with sand. Roughly two
months later, any that have not been dug up
and eaten by monitors, genets, mongooses,
hyenas or baboons hatch and the baby
crocodiles, heading for the water, face a new
array of enemies—including larger crocs.
Only the lucky will survive. While sunning
during the day, crocodiles regulate their body
temperature by opening their jaws. Evaporation
from the moist mouth lining cools them off.*

*A herd of Burchell's zebra gathers at a water hole in Namibia's Etosha National Park to drink, play, nurse the young
and socialize. Burchell's zebra divide along geographical lines from north to south into three main subspecies: Grant's
(or Boehm's), Selous and Chapman's. The differences consist almost entirely of color and striping variations.*

White-throated bee-eaters catch a pair of moths. One of some twenty-five species of bee-eaters—so named because their diet consists mostly of bees, hornets and wasps which they devour with impunity—the white-throated bee-eater thrives in a variety of habitats from the forest's edge to bush country and savanna. It can be distinguished from other bee-eaters by its elongated central tail feathers, black and white head markings and its cinnamon-colored underwings.

124

Birds of a feather flock to... water. The openbill stork (top) feeds on large water snails and molluscs. The little egret (lower left) can be found in all watery areas throughout Africa, as can cattle egrets (lower right) which sometimes gather in large numbers in the branches of dead trees when they aren't standing around on the backs of elephants or buffalo. The Goliath heron (opposite page), largest of Africa's herons, may stand five feet tall. A colony of these giants nests on Gibraltar Island in Kenya's Lake Baringo.

126

The Lilies of the Field

THE FISHER KING

The gull-like cry of the African fish eagle rings through many parts of East and Central Africa as the raptor hunts along rivers, lakes, swamps and other watery areas. It lives mainly on fish, but will also take an occasional rodent or other waterbird.

Its pattern of stripes and spots has earned the shy bushbuck the nickname "harnessed antelope." It inhabits savanna and forest areas throughout much of sub-Saharan Africa, always remaining near water. Most active during early morning and late afternoon or evening hours, it has become stealthy and nocturnal where hunted. It swims well and, although of relatively diminutive size at about three and a half feet in height, can leap a six and a half foot fence with ease.

Fastest animal on four feet, the cheetah can attain speeds up to seventy miles per hour over short distances in pursuit of prey. Their coloration and coat pattern make them difficult for potential quarry to see.

Male cheetahs often live, hunt and travel in pairs. Females tend to be solitary—a definite hazard for cubs when mother goes off hunting. In her absence, they may fall prey to other predators, or she may even forget where she left them. The males mark their territory by spraying trees or shrubs from anal glands. They play and groom each other until hunger drives them once again to hunt. On patrol, they use fallen trees, termite mounds or any elevated vantage point to scan the landscape for prey. Unlike all other cats, cheetahs cannot retract their claws.

The Cape or black buffalo has been widely accorded the honor of being Africa's most dangerous animal. Standing as much as six feet at the shoulder and weighing up to a ton, they have formidable horns and irascible dispositions that incline them to charge when irritated, let alone attacked. They have only one enemy apart from man—lions. Widely hunted as trophies or for meat and leather, they remain abundant and can be found in a wide variety of habitats from Lake Chad in the north to Africa's southern tip at the Cape of Good Hope and east to west between Senegal and Ethiopia.

Few people look upon the marabou stork as one of nature's noblest creatures. Ugly to the point of being piteous, the marabou (sometimes called adjutant because of its stiff, strutting gait) occupies a valuable place on the African janitorial staff, cleaning up carrion and helping to control locusts. The pink, air-filled pouch that hangs from adults' necks has no known function.

Without these mostly unloved and unlovely creatures, the African plains would be littered with the rotting corpses of the dead. Few animals display their greedy appetites as grossly as the vultures. Massed on an abandoned kill, their beaks clacking like castanets while they hiss and fight over every scrap, they make an unpleasant picture. In this unusual photograph, they have been joined on a wildebeest carcass by seventeen spotted hyenas and a single black-backed jackal. Together with marabou storks, who should be dropping in at any moment, they play a vital role in the health of the entire ecological community. A large dead animal such as a buffalo, giraffe or elephant might lie around decomposing for months, but with this efficient and industrious crew on the job their remains will be gone, bones and all, in no time.

Some seven species of vultures patrol the African savannas in search of carrion. Most numerous are the nearly identical white-backed and Ruppell's vultures (top and bottom insets) which gather in large numbers wherever a corpse can be found. Larger, rarer and considerably more spectacular, the lappet-faced or Nubian vulture (center insert and right) has a body length of more than three feet and an immense seven-foot wingspan on which it can soar at altitudes of several thousand feet for hours. Once on the ground, a vulture's aerial grace vanishes as it runs toward the corpse with wings and neck outstretched. Their only song consists of harsh croaking squawks.

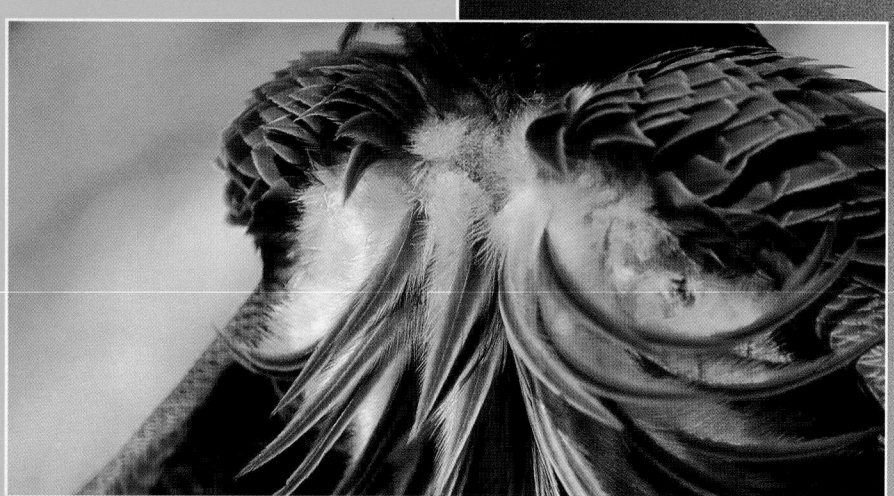

A spotted hyena, emerging from its den, snarls menacingly on finding itself unexpectedly confronted. Unlike vultures, the hyena and black-backed jackal hunt live prey. One of the hyena's many vocalizations, often employed after a successful hunt, resembles hysterical laughter; hence the expression, "laughing hyena." They usually live in pairs, but hunt in packs. Brutal and efficient predators with jaws powerful enough to crush large bones, they will in fact eat almost anything. Jackals, when not darting among the vultures and hyenas to steal a choice scrap, will also eat everything from eggs to berries. Fiercely tenacious, they will battle the same vultures who have driven lions or cheetahs from their kills.

MOSI-OA-TUNYA
"the smoke that thunders"

World's sixth largest cataract by volume, Victoria Falls on the Zambezi River consists of five separate falls ranging in height from 200 to 355 feet. A mean annual 35,400 cubic feet of water per second plunge into the narrow gorge below. Water vapor rising to more than 1,600 feet gives the place its African name of "smoke that thunders."

Mekoro (plural of **mokoro** and meaning dugout canoes), poled by expert guides, carry visitors through the Okavango Delta, a vast wetland in the heart of Botswana's Kalahari desert. The water of the Okavango River, rising from a spring in the highlands of Angola where it begins life as the Cubango River, travels more than a thousand miles before fanning out into the world's largest inland delta and ultimately disappearing into the desert sands. Enormous enough to be visible from space, it spreads over 8,500 square miles—home to an unequalled diversity of wildlife. Under the scorching Kalahari sun, ninety five percent of the delta's water evaporates every year, but with the swelling of new floods, it can double in size in just a few months. Rare red lechwe antelope roam the **molapos** (flooded grasslands) along with herds of buffalo numbering in the thousands, perhaps the largest concentration of these animals left on the continent.

151

In the watery wilderness of Okavango, a reed frog warms itself in the afternoon sun. It takes six months for seasonal rain water from the river's source in the Angolan highlands to arrive in the Okavango delta. As a result, the delta becomes wettest during the Kalahari's dry season—a fortuitous quirk of nature.

154

*Betty Morris (above) rides in a **mokoro** while Bebe walks alongside. Such up close and personal encounters sustain the elephants' reputation as gentle giants. A mahout watches while his charge rejoices in a cool bath.*

*Abu, Bebe and Kathy head out from Abu's Camp into Botswana's Okavango Delta with **Focus On Africa** members aboard. Baby elephants, orphaned by culling operations elsewhere, tag along. Randall Moore, former elephant trainer, turtle expert and now chief wrangler for Ker & Downey's elephant back safaris, brought these three pachyderms home to Africa from various zoos and circuses in America in 1989.*

If a thing of beauty really is a joy forever, the crowned crane certainly qualifies with its striking head of red, black and white topped with a golden crown. The predatory secretary bird, so-called because of the clutch of quills sticking out from the back of its head like so many pens, kills snakes, rodents and large insects for a living. The mournful marabou stork gives new meaning to the expression "homely as a hedge fence."

The Good, The Bad And The Ugly

Sex On The Savanna

The mating dance of the regal crowned crane combines stately elegance and dignity. Males and females look alike, but the offspring appear somewhat less dressy during their early lives.

Tallest of animals, a full-grown giraffe may stand eighteen feet from hoof to nose at full stretch. The reticulated variety, seen in these pictures, differs in pattern from the more common and wide-spread Masai giraffe. One of nature's most bizarre creatures, they have extremely long, prehensile black tongues with which they browse among the lethal thorns of acacia trees, eating only the tender new leaves and shoots. Their immense size and graceful if peculiar gait create an impression of slow motion, but at full gallop they can attain speeds of thirty-five miles per hour and outrun a horse. The power in a defensive kick from one of their hind legs can send a full-grown lion flying. Their calves, after gestating for almost fifteen months, emerge all neck and legs and plunge four or five feet to the ground—a rude introduction to life. Gentle and sociable by nature, they often keep company with groups of zebra, wildebeest or ostrich.

Last of a once larger race of giant flightless birds that included the huge extinct moa of New Zealand, the ostrich now reigns as the largest living bird. Fully grown, it may stand eight feet high and weigh up to 345 pounds. Their powerful legs and two-toed feet propel them at speeds up to thirty miles an hour and make deadly defensive weapons. An ostrich egg, encased in a thick, ivory-like shell and weighing up to three pounds, takes more than forty days to incubate. Cock and hen share incubation duty, but the cock takes charge of the chicks after birth. Their feathers have long been popular as dusters and they are sometimes raised like domestic fowl on ostrich ranches.

FACES IN THE CROWD

Everyone looks, but few are lucky enough to see the elusive leopard in the course of a short safari. They hunt at night and hide by day. Their great strength enables them to haul a heavy antelope into the trees for leisurely dining away from marauding scavengers. Among the most beautiful of the big cats, their skins once brought big prices in the days when wild animal fur was considered de rigueur. Current estimates suggest that there may be as many as 100,000 leopards remaining in all of Africa.

169

The waterbuck, sometimes also called
Defassa, frequents large areas of East,
Central and South Africa, grazing the
savannas and gallery forests near water.
Luckily for this animal, predators do
not consider the adults a favorite menu
choice because of their tough, stringy,
rank-scented meat. When hunted, they
take to the water, defending themselves
with formidable horns or hiding in
reeds submerged up to the nose.

170

"Poems are made by fools like me,
But only God can make a tree…"
Joyce Kilmer

And in Africa, He made some strange ones—like the sausage tree (upper left), and the baobab (opposite page), sometimes called the upside down tree. The stupendous girth of a baobab dwarfs Janice Bartlett. The Doum palm delights photographers with its graceful shapes and the acacia (bottom) is Africa's signature tree.

Bird-watchers paradise: Africa, so well-known for the so-called "big five" game animals, also boasts a nearly unparalleled variety of birds. With a little planning, visitors might see more than two-hundred fifty species in a single day including, perhaps, the vulturine guineafowl (opposite page), the African hoopoe, kori bustard and eastern double-collared sunbird (left, top to bottom) or the lilac-breasted roller, two-banded courser and the European roller (right, top to bottom).

"Ji, ji, ji, jeeee" chatters the grey-headed kingfisher, one of about fourteen species of this large family of fish- and insect-eating birds found in Africa. The grey-headed kingfisher inhabits dry country, feeding on lizards and large insects. Their heads and bills seem out of proportion to their stubby wings and bodies, but their predatory skills hardly suffer on that account. Plunging from a tree branch, their attack is swift and deadly.

THE WEAVERS

At Gibb's Farm, situated on a hill overlooking coffee plantations between Lake Manyara and Ngorongoro Crater in Tanzania, grosbeak weaver birds construct their elaborate nests from vegetative fiber. In some other weaver species, a single nest may contain hundreds of females rearing their young. Occasionally, the weight of such a nest causes the supporting tree to collapse.

DRAGONS OF EDEN

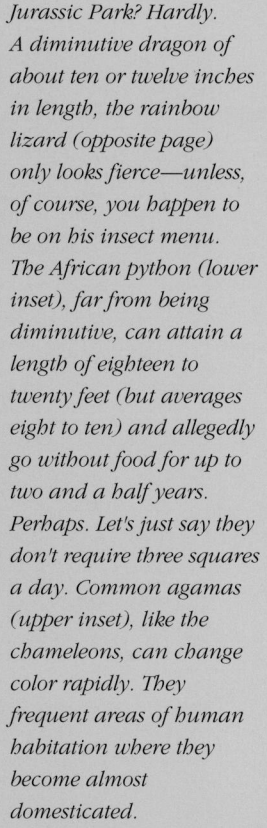

A velociraptor from Jurassic Park? Hardly. A diminutive dragon of about ten or twelve inches in length, the rainbow lizard (opposite page) only looks fierce—unless, of course, you happen to be on his insect menu. The African python (lower inset), far from being diminutive, can attain a length of eighteen to twenty feet (but averages eight to ten) and allegedly go without food for up to two and a half years. Perhaps. Let's just say they don't require three squares a day. Common agamas (upper inset), like the chameleons, can change color rapidly. They frequent areas of human habitation where they become almost domesticated.

Namib-Naukluft National Park

Wilderness of red sand, the searing inferno of the Namib desert bakes in the equatorial sun. Among the world's oldest deserts, its hostile environment still supports a considerable variety of life, including the astonishing **welwitschia mirabilis** (second from bottom inset). Some of these peculiar trees were growing here while Jesus preached in Galilee, making them among the oldest living things on earth. In places, particularly the area called Sossusvlei at the southern end of the park, the dunes rise to heights of more than a thousand feet, dwarfing men and their vehicles. Petroglyphs testify to the presence of man at least four-thousand— perhaps even as much as ten-thousand years ago. Survival here requires constant struggle against a harsh and unforgiving environment, as dead trees and the bleaching skull of an elephant eloquently remind us. The consolidation of the Namib Desert and Naukluft Mountain Zebra National Parks into Namib-Naukluft created one of the largest and perhaps one of the most unusual parks in the world.

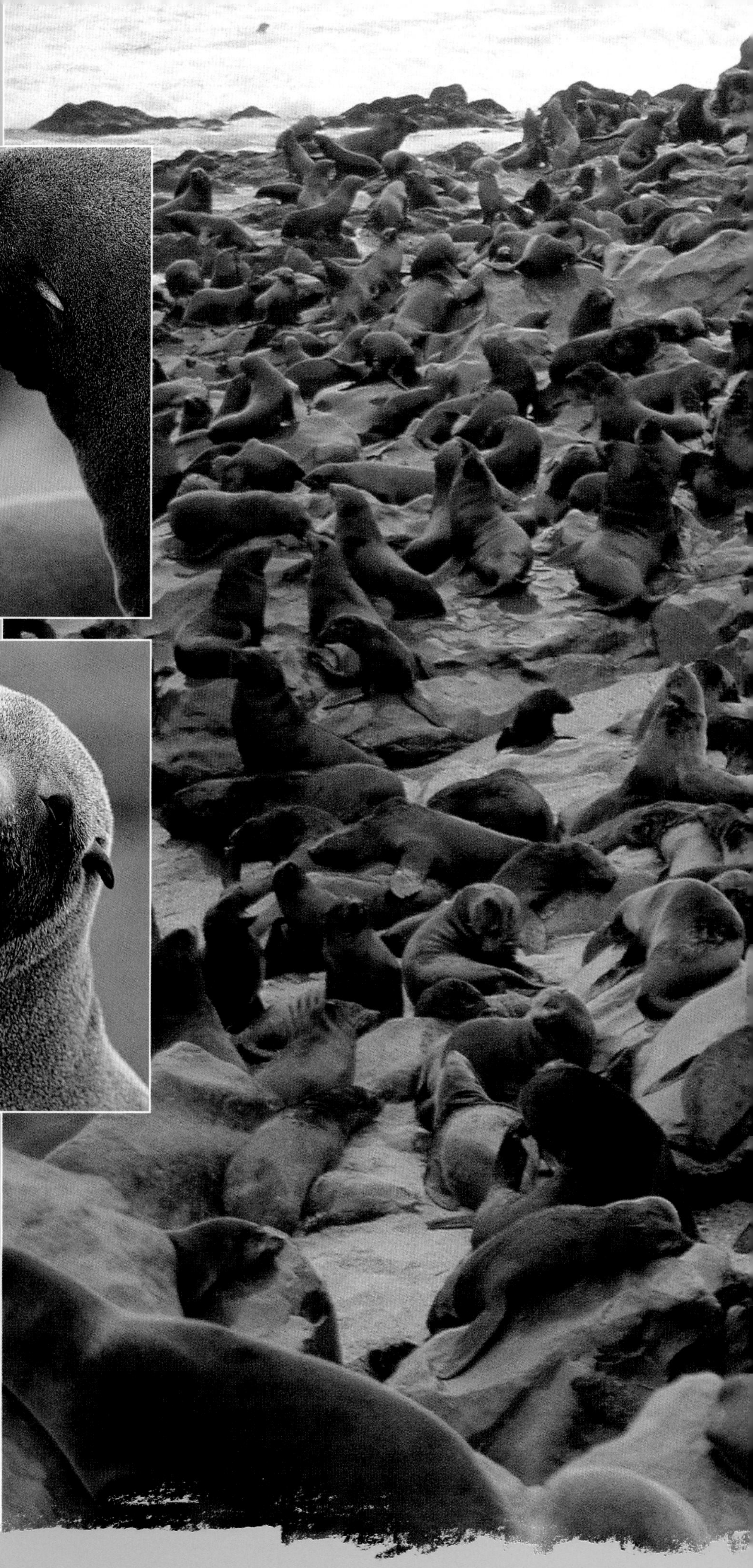

On the beach at Cape Cross, Namibia, a throng of Cape fur seals sun themselves and tend the young. Unlike true seals, these animals possess external, readily visible ears. Their coats, consisting of an outer layer of coarse guard hairs and a dense undercoat of luxuriant fur, protect them against the cold waters in which they spend most of their lives. Unfortunately, those same coats had the opposite effect on men, who slaughtered them to the brink of extinction for their fur. Today, strict protection has allowed their numbers to revive.

184

In Zimbabwe's Matopos National Park, local villages take seasonal turns harvesting grass inside the park for repairing and thatching roofs. In this way, the park returns some benefit to the people who live around it.

Danger in the grass: the food chain revealed. Three lions on the prowl may bring down a topi (lower left inset). When they're finished, vultures will clean up the remains and so, what goes around comes around—in nature's harsh but efficient economy.

"So long and thanks for coming. Please drop by again soon and bring your friends."

ON SAFARI

The safari experience has undergone considerable change since the days of the Great White Hunters. No one today gathers up an army of porters, gun bearers, tent boys and soldiers before heading into the bush on foot to shoot big game. Modern hunters, whether armed with cameras or rifles, stalk their quarry in customized vehicles and sacrifice very few of the civilized amenities they're accustomed to. Teddy Roosevelt's mammoth expedition in 1909 might seem like the epitome of roughing it from a 1990's perspective, but he felt that "our tents, our accommodations generally, seemed almost too comfortable for men who knew camp life only on the Great Plains, in the Rockies, and in the North Woods." "Old Rough and Ready" would scoff at the level of luxury available on most safaris today. Even so, from the notes and diaries turned in by the *Focus On Africa* participants it's clear that misconceptions about what to expect on safari in Africa remain widespread. Mention a "tented camp" and the image that usually springs to mind bears scant resemblance to such places as Samburu Intrepids where the furnishings would put many a cosmopolitan luxury hotel to shame. The sight of a pair of four-poster canopied beds gracing a green canvas tent in the bush is quietly dumbfounding. Not every tented camp can compare to Samburu Intrepids of course, but few if any match the somewhat Spartan conditions most people think of as tent camping. They bear just enough resemblance to that notion to invoke the romance of roughing it without the inconvenience or discomfort.

Since 1978 I have personally led more than fifty safaris. In that time I've had many adventures and unique experiences. On one rainy day, not far from

Governors' Camp in the Masai Mara, a group of our vans had become mired in the mud. This particular safari had been dogged by the kind of capricious misfortunes every tour operator dreads—more annoying than serious. Standing in the pouring rain, up to my ankles in muck, I lapsed into an uncharacteristically somber mood. Suddenly a band of Maasai *Ilmoran* (warriors) appeared, looking fierce and bristling with spears. They eyed the situation and decided we needed help. As they walked by, one growled to me, "Here, hold my spear." Without further fanfare, they literally picked the vehicles up, moved them to dry ground, retrieved their weapons, and continued on their way. I laughed about that for the rest of the trip.

Every safari is made up of such experiences. For each individual, the surprises are many and different. Not all are pleasant, of course. Life is never that consistent, but no one is ever bored. Even an experience like mine in the mud loses in retrospect whatever negative edge it might have had at the time. With *Focus On Africa's* one-hundred thirty-six people taking twenty-five different itineraries over sixteen weeks to eight countries, we anticipated a certain number of problems and disappointments. Life is, after all, impossible to control in every detail, and Africa is a huge Third World place with a lot of really bad roads. The surprise wasn't how many things went wrong; it was that so few did.

Of all our twenty-five itineraries, Ker & Downey's elephant back safari in Botswana's Okavango Delta clearly stands out as uniquely special. It is certainly among the most remarkable trips you can take anywhere in the world. At a place called Abu's Camp, on the banks of the Xhenega River, an American expatriate from Oregon named Randall Moore has made a specialty out of being an elephant wrangler. Moore has had an unconventional career. After training circus elephants for a few years, he became a wildlife biologist and an expert on Mexico's endangered sea turtles. But then he chucked all that to escort three African elephants home. Four more elephants eventually followed and three of the seven now carry Randall's guests through the Okavango Delta. Abu's Camp can only accommodate ten people at a time, so those lucky enough to take the elephant back safari become members of a pretty exclusive club.

People on safari often express a strong desire to get closer to the wildlife. When they come upon a pride of lions with several cubs, they are apt to be seized by an irrepressible desire to get out of the van and pet one. Naturally, this would be ill-advised. The wild animals of Africa are just that—wild. We are the visitors, the ones who must be caged. Nevertheless, this urge to get closer affects almost everyone and understandably so. For those who absolutely must gratify it, Ker & Downey's elephant back safari gets you as up close and personal as anyone could want, short of sticking your head in the lion's mouth. You can ride through the Okavango marshes on mighty Abu's back, walk among the herd (which includes several babies orphaned by culling) and even take a refreshing swim with these amazingly gentle pachyderms. If predators should appear—say a lion or a pack of wild dogs—Randall will advise you to "tuck into the herd" because, as one guest put it, "when you're riding with the elephants, you're riding with the A-Team, heavy-weight division."

As we noted previously, primates often show up live in local meat markets where they are sold for food at what seem incredibly low prices to the horrified Western mind. At the Mount Kenya Game Ranch, we made the acquaintance of a five and a half year-old male chimpanzee rescued from such a market by Karl Ammann who paid $8 for him. This beguiling animal, called Mzee [old man], because of his wrinkly face, produced an astonishing effect on the members of our group. Anya Cristina Stout, a young, well-traveled woman from New York, formed an instant bond with him and displayed as much or more affection as she might have for an orphaned child. So did my son, Jason. It certainly wasn't hard to see why. It would be difficult to imagine a more appealing or affectionate animal than Mzee. Looking into his eyes, Jason said, felt like looking into the eyes of another human being.

Of course, every safari is unique in its own way, and each individual's experience of it will be determined by the sum of their particular impressions and desires. In their own words, the *Focus On Africa* people had these things to say about their adventures On Safari:

"I will never forget the gracious spirit of Africa's people, the elegance of the wildlife, and the majestic plains…"

—Paula Adams

"Most people think Africa is hot and dry, and full of bugs! Little do they know it's the most fabulous zoo in the world. The animals, in their environment, are too incredible for words. The vastness of the place, the diversity of the landscape, the wonderful people all make Africa a wonderful place to visit."

—Pam Pullen

"We slept to an orchestra of lions' mournful roars and hippos' grunting laughter, eagerly accompanied by the resonating brass section of distant elephants. The morning mist dances with the mighty Zambezi as the sun floats above the horizon reflecting images of African dreams. It was fun and exciting to be part of such an ambitious and worthwhile project. A life-changing adventure!"

—Janice O. Bartlett

"One of the drivers summed up the whole trip for me in this sentence: 'The word safari does not mean simply to make a journey, but rather to experience the things you have never experienced before.' I can't think of a better place than Africa to do that."

—Daphne Polson

"Before I died I wanted to see and feel Africa. Now and only now can I truly live!"

—Dianne Henderson

"I went to Africa with the hope that by getting closer to nature in the cradle of civilization I would find a way to become closer to God. I was pleased that the spiritual awakening which I experienced during those three and a half months of safaris far exceeded my expectations. I found what I was seeking, and I believe that I will forever be a happier and better person because of these African experiences."

—Edward A. Morris

"As an attorney of 14 years, there is no other occasion that I can remember warranting so many superlatives to describe one event."

—Kathy B. Gregg

"While on an afternoon game drive at M'bali, we were stunned to see a native out jogging! (It was after sundown and night had fallen.) It turns out our radio wasn't working properly and he was relaying a message to us about a sighting. The native's participation was heart-warming and made the trip better."

—Richard F. Reber

"What started as a vacation to photograph new things turned into a quest to help save the wildlife. This was my first trip ever in 48 years out of North America and it was a wonderful adventure."

—Michael M. Sheras

"The obvious delight the people felt in our being there plus their determination to keep us comfortable, happy and well-fed made it doubly delightful."

—Sharon Hackley

"I came away feeling diminished by the vastness and beauty of the country and animals and the creativity of the African people. My perspective on American 'superiority' has changed. I find myself mentally wandering to the unspoiled life of Kenya."

—Guy Biegler

"Call it something other than 'tourism.' This African adventure is not given justice when it is referred to as a tour. No tour could live up to this type of experience."

—Barry Bartolacci

"Each time I arrive back in Africa, I feel like I have come home. Each time I fly out of the last game area, I cry."

—Esther Lidstrom

"I am very interested in contributing to the world wide effort of conserving our past and our future cultural and wildlife heritages and can think of no better way."

—Nancy McCarthy

"We must convince Americans that the people of Africa wear clothes and are not poor – they are only poor by our standards. In reality they are rich because even though they have little compared to us, they are happy and they have everything they need because nature provides it. Money from other people is not necessary to be happy."

—R. David Cobb

"While so much will be said about the land and animals, I want to express my thanks at having had an opportunity to meet and share time with such intelligent, interesting, and vital people. Each person I met along the way has added to my knowledge and friendships and appreciation of the diversity of life."

—Mary A. Nelson

"May 21st—a day of babies... the lion cubs, the newborn giraffe and his concerned family members, the large 'liquid' eyes of the baby hyena. The nights — such noise. The sunsets — they really are that red. And the elephants in the river."

—Sylvia A. Hosie

"The trackers cutting a curtain of vines and revealing 'Ninja' [a silverback male mountain gorilla]—all 800 lbs. of him—eight feet from my camera. Sunset on a kopje in the Serengeti with silver service cocktails while the wildebeest migrated at our feet and lions roared in the distance."

—Robert M. Fairbanks

"Our safari group sat in two open Land Rovers in a small clearing at night. The spotlight was on a lioness resting in the middle of the clearing. The spillover from the spotlight softly lit the trees around the clearing. The sky was covered with stars which seemed almost close enough to touch. The night was cool and stimulating. There is no way to totally describe the scene or my enjoyment."

—Preston B. Ozmar

"After two trips to Africa on safari, the opportunity to return with a purpose (not just as a tourist) thrilled me. South Africa has so much to offer—I hope the political situation will not destroy it. It was not as bad as our press has reported. I wish everyone could have this experience. It makes you appreciate our wonderful world and all of the wonders in it. I just hope that the animals will continue to thrive... There has to be a way they can co-exist and hopefully this project will do just that."

—Sandra Yon

"I am so grateful to have been able to participate in this incredible safari experience. I am forever a changed woman as a result."

—Anya Cristina Stout

"We both can't wait to go back. I don't think either one of us has come down from the high. I hope I never do! The people were so nice everywhere we went. This trip was the best thing I have ever done in my entire life."

—Mary Sesto &
Margaret Borich

"The entire trip was not a vacation, but rather an emotional happening from the school girls [AIC Girls Primary School] to seeing the most magnificent collection of wildlife and scenery. I came to see cheetah and I did. I cried!"

—Steve Casper

"Seeing 24 elephants at dusk—a happy family enjoying each other, babies nursing and then playing with each other, trunks intertwined, basking in the glory of living."

—Bonnie Casper

"Desire to return, to know more about the people, the economics, the wildlife. Some compulsion to see Africa again as it is in a changing state and what I experienced may not be easily captured again."

—Gail Molzahn

"I have never been on a trip as wonderful as this. Even though my safari was only 2 weeks long, it was the trip of a lifetime for me. The opportunity to see animals in the wild instead of behind bars is something everyone should experience…"

—Carlo Quaia

"Words to describe Africa are difficult to come by. The one that comes to my mind most often is vast. One certainly is aware of one's smallness in this vast land."

—Virginia Rider

The Photographers

Edmond Alexander
Santa Rosa Beach, Florida
May 15 - 27; Botswana

Steve & Linda Alexander
Fayetteville, New York
March 18 - 25; Tanzania

Natalie Brecher
Redondo Beach, California
March 26 - April 8; Kenya

Christine Campbell
Cornelius, Oregon
March 26 - April 5; Kenya

Robert Cushman
Dalton, Georgia
March 18 - 25; Tanzania

Eugene Davis
Newberg, Oregon
April 26 - June 7; Namibia, Botswana, Zimbabwe

Janet Gorski
Highlands Ranch, Colorado
March 18 - April 8; Tanzania, Kenya

Jessie Harris
Washington, D.C.
June 12 - 25; Botswana

Brian Hastings
Santa Barbara, California
April 26 - May 16 and May 30 - June 7; Namibia, South Africa

Gregg Hyman
Oakland, California
June 7 - 20; Zambia

Marilyn Iannarelli
La Grange Park, Illinois
April 9 - 21; Zaire, Botswana

Richard Jarvi
Richmond, Maine
June 20 - July 3; Zimbabwe

196

Paul Lee
Renton, Washington
March 26 - April 8;
Kenya

Esther Lidstrom
Sayville, New York
June 20 - July 3;
Zimbabwe

Herb Lundin
Huntington Beach,
California
June 7 - 20; Zambia

Nancy McCarthy
Pipersville, Pennsylvania
June 20 - July 3;
Zimbabwe

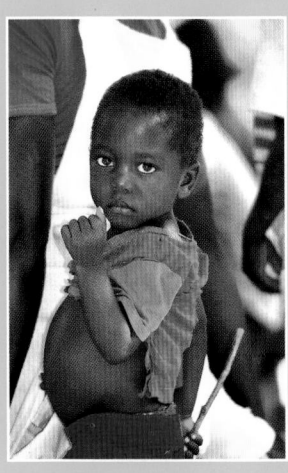

Nancy Nevin
Annandale, Virginia
May 15 - June 7;
Botswana, Zimbabwe

Myra Nunley
Ventura, California
June 13 - 20; Tanzania

Daphne Polson
Westlake, Ohio
March 18 - April 13;
Tanzania, Kenya, Zaire

Portia Racasi
New York, New York
March 26 - April 13;
Kenya, Zaire

Ed Snoke
Elkhart, Indiana
April 5 - 13; Kenya,
Zaire

Kelly Stone
New York, New York
March 18 - April 8;
Tanzania, Kenya

Mark Van Bergh
Washington, D.C.
March 18 - April 5;
Tanzania, Kenya

Karen Vernon
Sydney, Australia
April 26 - May 16;
Namibia

Paula Adams
Long Beach, California
March 18 - April 5; Tanzania, Kenya

Eric Adler
Baltimore, Maryland
June 21 - July 1; Kenya

Marlan Adler
Baltimore, Maryland
June 21 - July 1; Kenya

Cynthia Turner Alexander
Santa Rosa Beach, Florida
May 15 - 27; Botswana

Tim Allen
Columbus, Ohio
June 21 - July 1; Kenya

David & Jason Anderson
Santa Barbara, California
*March 18 - July 1; Tanzania, Kenya,
Zaire, Botswana, Namibia, Zimbabwe,
Zambia*

198

Gail Anderson
Santa Barbara, California
*April 5 - 13 and May 27 - June 7;
Kenya, Zaire, Zimbabwe*

Arledge Armenaki
Canoga Park, California
March 18 - 25; Tanzania

Janice Bartlett
Cardiff, California
June 7 - 20; Zambia

Barry Bartolacci
Dallas, Texas
June 20 - July 3; Zimbabwe

Ron Berchin
San Francisco, California
June 7 - 20; Zambia

Guy & Rosemary Biegler
Saratoga Springs, New York,
March 26 - April 13; Kenya, Zaire

David Bridge
Rancho Santa Fe, California
March 18 - April 8; Tanzania, Kenya

Tim Bundgard
Boise, Idaho
June 21 - July 1; Kenya

Peter Caine
New South Wales, Australia
March 26 - April 8; Kenya

Bonnie Casper
Cincinnati, Ohio
March 18 - 25; Tanzania

Steve Casper
Cincinnati, Ohio
March 18 - 25; Tanzania

Mary Jane Headlee Clevenger
Santa Barbara, California
June 20 - July 3; Zimbabwe

Ralph Clevenger
Santa Barbara, California
June 20 - July 3; Zimbabwe

R. David Cobb
Lexington, Kentucky
June 7 - 20; Zambia

Alan Cutler
Chicago, Illinois
June 20 - July 3; Zimbabwe

Eileen Day
Chicago, Illinois
June 20 - July 3; Zimbabwe

Julie de Kock
Solvang, California
June 13 - 20; Tanzania

Joseph Denker
Studio City, California
June 13 - July 1; Tanzania, Kenya

THE PHOTOGRAPHERS (Continued)

P. Michael Dodds
Northridge, California
June 21 - July 1; Kenya

Glenna Evans
Chicago, Illinois
March 18 - April 13; Tanzania, Kenya, Zaire

Paul Mark Evans
Chicago, Illinois
March 26 - April 13; Kenya, Zaire

Patricia Fairbanks
Dana Point, California
March 18 - April 26; Tanzania, Kenya, Zaire, Botswana

Robert Fairbanks
Dana Point, California
March 18 - April 26; Tanzania, Kenya, Zaire, Botswana

Thomas Field
Noblesville, Indiana
March 26 - April 8; Kenya

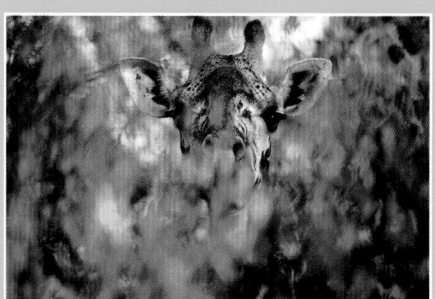

David Friedner
New York, New York
April 5 - 8; Kenya

Barbara Galbraith
Dallas, Texas
April 26 - May 16; Namibia

James Galbraith
Dallas, Texas
April 26 - May 16; Namibia

Charles A. Graham
Carpinteria, California
May 15 - 27; Botswana

Kathy Gregg & Richard Reber
Bal Harbour, Florida
May 30 - June 7; South Africa

Robert & Jackie Grigg
Elmhurst, Illinois
March 18 - April 5; Tanzania, Kenya

Chuck Gutierrez
Boonton Township, New Jersey
June 21 - July 1; Kenya

Kate Gutierrez
Boonton Township, New Jersey
June 21 - July 1; Kenya

Sharon Hackley
Kingman, Arizona
June 20 - July 3; Zimbabwe

Charles & Annick Hall
Miami, Florida
May 30 - June 7; South Africa

Donna Hands
Davis, California.
June 7 - 30; Zambia, South Africa

Dianne Henderson
Santa Maria, California
April 5 - 13; Kenya, Zaire

201

Jane Hoffer
New York, New York
March 26 - April 5; Kenya

Andrew Horton
Santa Barbara, California
*March 18 - June 20; Tanzania, Kenya,
Zaire, Botswana, Namibia, Zambia*

Sylvia Hosie
Newport, Oregon
May 15 - 27; Botswana

Edward Hotchkiss
New York, New York
May 15 - 27; Botswana

Marvin Jetton
Bel Air, Texas
March 18 - 25; Tanzania

Beverly Johnson
Pulaksi, Tennessee
April 5 - 21; Kenya, Zaire, Botswana

David Johnson
Pulaksi, Tennessee
April 5 - 21; Kenya, Zaire, Botswana

Raymond Kammer
Naperville, Illinois
April 26 - May 16; Namibia

Patricia Kelly
Birmingham, Alabama
June 12 - 25; Botswana

Kim Kirkland
Birmingham, Alabama
April 5 - 8; Kenya

Dorothy Kuhne
Santa Barbara, California
March 26 - April 8; Kenya

Lin Legum
Virginia Beach, Virginia
June 12 - 25; Botswana

202

Mary Lundin
Huntington Beach, California
June 7 - 20; Zambia

Mike Luppino
New York, New York
March 26 - April 13; Kenya, Zaire

Anthony Marturano
Los Angeles, California
March 18 - April 8; Tanzania, Kenya

Karen McGougan
Lucas, Texas
March 18 - 25; Tanzania

Gail Molzahn
Downers Grove, Illinois
March 18 - April 8; Tanzania, Kenya

Roger Molzahn
Downers Grove, Illinois
March 18 - April 8; Tanzania, Kenya

Edward & Betty Morris
San Francisco, California
*March 18 - June 30; Tanzania, Kenya,
Zaire, Botswana, Namibia, Zimbabwe,
South Africa*

Mary Ann Nelson
Baton Rouge, Louisiana
*May 27 - June 14; Zimbabwe, South
Africa*

Rosemary Nevin
Annandale, Virginia
May 15 - June 7; Botswana, Zimbabwe

Erwin (Bud) Nielson
Tucson, Arizona
April 9 - 13; Zaire

Richard Nunley
Ventura, California
June 13 - 20; Tanzania

Cheryl Opperman
Littleton, Colorado
March 18 - April 8; Tanzania, Kenya

203

Judy Ozmar
Virginia Beach, Virginia
June 20 - 30; South Africa

Preston Ozmar
Virginia Beach, Virginia
June 20 - 30; South Africa

Mary Patton
Santa Rosa Beach, Florida
May 15 - 27; Botswana

Tom Patton
Santa Rosa Beach, Florida
May 15 - 27; Botswana

Susan Peterson
Grandview, Missouri
June 20 - July 3; Zimbabwe

Pam Pullen
Birmingham, Alabama
June 12 - 25; Botswana

THE PHOTOGRAPHERS (Continued)

Carlo Quaia
Vancouver, British Columbia, Canada
March 26 - April 5; Kenya

Tom Rasmussen
Redondo Beach, California
March 26 - April 8; Kenya

Daryl Rice
Perkasie, Pennsylvania
June 20 - July 3; Zimbabwe

Raimar Richers
São Paulo, Brasil
June 21 - July 1; Kenya

Virginia Rider
Renton, Washington
March 26 - April 5; Kenya

J. Melvin Sauerbeck
Chappaqua, New York
April 26 - May 16; Namibia

Samuel Saylor
Dumont, New Jersey
March 18 - April 5; Tanzania, Kenya

Mary Jane Sesto
Torrence, California
May 30 - June 7; South Africa

Michael Sheras
Alexandria, Virginia
June 21 - July 1; Kenya

Ellen Silbermann
New York, New York
April 21 - 26; Botswana

Shirley Sochor
Arlington Heights, Illinois
April 15 - 26; Botswana

David Soong
Los Angeles, California
*May 27 - June 7 and June 20 - July 3;
Zimbabwe, Zambia*

Ann Anthony Stanley
Little Rock, Arkansas
March 18 - 25; Tanzania

Rebecca Stebbins
Santa Barbara, California
June 21 - July 1; Kenya

Anya Cristina Stout
Purdys, New York
*April 15 - 26 and June 13 - July 1;
Botswana, Tanzania, Kenya*

Jay Thamert
Kent, Washington
March 26 - April 8; Kenya

Mary Tong
Oakland, California
June 7 - 20; Zambia

Maxine Valdez
Riverside, California
June 20 - 30; South Africa

205

Michael & Ruth Verbois
Santa Barbara, California
*March 18 - April 13; Tanzania, Kenya,
Zaire*

Raymond Watt
Glendale, California
April 26 - May 16; Namibia

Steve Welsh
Boise, Idaho
June 21 - July 1; Kenya

Larry White
Mt. Vernon, Ohio
April 26 - May 16; Namibia

C.J. Wills
Novi, Missouri
March 26 - April 5; Kenya

Sandra Yon
Virginia Beach, Virginia
June 20 - 30; South Africa

BEN KIPENO – *Maasai village chief and Friends of Conservation Masai Mara community conservation extension officer*

Education is the key. You of *Focus On Africa* came to learn what is happening in Kenya. If you write about us and your visit to our kraal, people all over the world will read it and that will be good for our tribe. We don't want to remain enclosed. We must learn about other people and what is happening in other places. We want other people to learn about us.

KARL AMMANN – *photographer, tourism consultant, book and film producer*

It has been realized worldwide, especially in Africa, that wildlife has to earn its keep one way or the other—either through cropping and the sale of meat which will give farmers income, or through tourism which is probably the most beneficial way. Without direct benefits, the local populations see very little reason for keeping the wildlife around. Tourism is one of the very few ways there can be a direct return from wildlife for the local people.

We first became involved with chimpanzees when we encountered one for sale on a boat in the Congo. Out of compassion, we bought it. Bringing it here to Kenya was very involved. Once you do become involved with chimps, you quickly realize that they are very different from dogs and cats. However, having one for a pet for awhile is not fair because they live to be forty or fifty and they're likely to have a whole lifetime still ahead of them when they become so big and powerful that they have to be confined in cages. We talked to Dr. Leakey about setting up a sanctuary. He was somewhat skeptical, but encouraging. We then went to see other existing sanctuaries and compiled a report on what was feasible. Lonrho Hotels agreed to let us use Ol Pejeta ranch. At this point, we have integrated three animals into a two-acre electrically fenced enclosure where they can learn to interact and become chimps again.

We're in a very advantageous position in Kenya because we have tourism and we have the infrastructure for the chimps to be able to earn their living. If there is a proper colony that will behave and interact as they would in the wild in an open country like Ol Pejeta where people can actually observe them, tourists should be very interested— under the right guidance—to learn what chimps are all about. Other sanctuaries I have visited in places like the Congo Republic and Gambia have no real hope of ever

A VIEW FROM AFRICA

attracting any tourist income and to them it's just outgoing money. When the present keepers and the people who support these sanctuaries die, where is the money to operate them in the future going to come from? Who is going to take care of those forty or fifty animals? If no one is there to do it, what will happen to them?

Research on wild-ranging chimps in other parts of Africa is still possible, but some countries have such a terrible infrastructure that researchers won't even attempt to work in them. What I hope this facility of ours will achieve is to get a lot more people interested and committed to chimp conservation and that the chimps here will become ambassadors for the chimps in the countries where they are indigenous. In Sierra Leone I found about fifty chimps in captivity just in Freetown. I've never seen such horrible conditions. There is a female who has been locked in an outdoor toilet for three years who has gone berserk. These creatures are 98.6 percent genetically human. What gives us the right to treat them like that? If you did that to a retarded child there would be a huge outcry, but in many ways a chimp is not less human than a retarded child.

The main problem with orphaned chimps and gorillas has nothing to do with export for the pet trade or for labs. That has virtually stopped throughout most of Africa. Now it's just subsistence hunting. I paid eight dollars for a chimp in the Congo Republic. People criticized me for encouraging the trade, but that animal's meat value at two and a half kilos was eight dollars as well. If I hadn't picked it up and taken it to a sanctuary in Brazzaville, it would have ended up on the dinner table. I know one shouldn't pay for these animals, but in this case I think the eight dollars committed was in the interest of conservation.

AMBROSE GACHUI – *field naturalist, guide and conservationist since 1973*

Today, guides go through an intensive three-year college training period. When I started, there was only on-the-job training. Guiding involves all aspects of nature. You need to know about trees, animals, even insects. You also need to know quite a bit about people and their cultures, both visitors and locals. You have to understand human psychology. The amount and quality of information given out to a visitor can be as simple as "that's a lion" or "that's an elephant," or it can be expanded to become a fifteen-minute lecture on those animals. Field guides are like an encyclopedia; it's a continuous learning process.

Generally speaking, people should probably not be allowed to drive themselves around on a safari. In the old days, the game department had rangers at entry points to the national parks and reserves who were just direction guides. But now, with so many visitors, tours should be taken over by a professional guide who ensures that the rules and regulations are observed.

For animals to survive, Kenya and Africa in general must create revenue out of wildlife. The only way we can create that revenue, outside of organized game hunting, is through tourism, but it's a "catch-22" situation. Someone has to determine how many visitors are too many for one specific destination. Ten years ago, for example, we were saying that the Masai Mara had too many visitors, but now we know that the Mara can accommodate twenty times more visitors than it had then. The peripheral areas around the parks are also potential tourism destinations and we are talking of walking safaris, horseback riding, and other innovative things that have not yet been offered to visitors.

We need responsible administrators for the tourism traffic. The lodges and camps are easy to control because once the beds are full you cannot take any more visitors. But it is not just the number of visitors; it is how responsible the guides are in making sure that it doesn't look too crowded. A cheetah with fifteen mini-buses gathered around it isn't a result of too many tourists; it's a result of irresponsible or poorly trained guides and drivers.

With proper organization, you should be able to spend seventy-five percent of a typical ten-day safari's forty hours of game viewing alone—either as one of three or four mini-buses if you're on a group tour, or as an individual vehicle if you're out on a private safari. We have vast areas out there. If you see vehicles looking at something, you can wait until they move on. The problem is that a lot of the drivers are not qualified game trackers, so instead of looking for animals they look for vehicles that are looking at animals. The average time spent with a cheetah or a lion by most mini-buses is only five minutes. If you have two or three nights at a destination, you should be able to spend fifteen or twenty minutes without other vehicles around. People need to spend more time at the different destinations. It's the ones rushing through these one-night stops that are leading the drivers to cause traffic jams.

But we have come a long way. Efforts have been made, not only by individuals, but by organizations concerned about conservation in general and habitat and animal behavior in particular. The interaction between man and wildlife has always been there. The Maasai cohabitate with the wildlife very happily and respect each other's territory. We need to understand that animals, if they are going to be viewed to raise revenue to stop these areas from becoming farms and grazing land for commercial livestock, have to be inconvenienced somehow. We need to compromise between leaving them wild with no visitors and having them bothered by being visited and photographed. I appeal to people who have not been to Africa to come and see the beauty of the land and wildlife. That is the only way we can ensure that the animals will survive for the coming generations.

FARID SULEIMAN – *involved with wildlife for more than thirty years, professional guide for the past fifteen years*

I was born, raised and educated in Mombasa and count myself fortunate that I was brought up by an uncle who was a warden in Tsavo National Park for ten years. During my school holidays I would go and visit him and help to do some of the control work on elephants or buffalo or whatever else there was to do. From those times I developed a lifelong interest in wildlife. From the first, I wanted to get involved in the *Focus On Africa* project and be a part of this very worthwhile effort. All the feedback we have had so far from local people around Nairobi and Kenya in general who have heard about the project has been very positive. They see it as a wonderful opportunity to put things straight. The press lately has been very unfair to Kenya and to Africa as a whole and it's wonderful to have the *Focus On Africa* people here to help correct that negative image.

I first got into tourism in the mid-70s as a driver-guide. In those days I also did a lot of walking tours for the more energetic travelers who liked to get out, after all the bumpy rides on our super roads, and get the feel of the surroundings by walking among the friendly animals—like wildebeest and zebra—or down by the river to look at hippos and birdlife. There have been many changes since those days. The animals were afraid then because hunting was still permitted. The facilities, like Kichwa Tembo and all the other very comfortable lodges and hotels we have today, have also changed. Now people can come and stay in these wonderful places, go out on game drives in custom-made vehicles, and get closer to the animals than ever before, especially since hunting is no longer allowed and the animals are not so frightened. Recently, there has been a lot of talk about reintroducing controlled hunting and I have mixed feelings about that. If it remains controlled, I think it's an excellent idea

In the thirty years that I've been with wildlife, I've seen some populations go down and some go up. The wildebeest and most of the plains game have increased because of the establishment of the national parks and the improvement in the way they're run and patrolled. Meat poachers are no longer around. Rhino, on the other hand, have gone down very much because poachers want their horns which are worth quite a bit of money. But, with all the protection now going on, things are getting better.

I believe that tourism is certainly the best chance for Africa's wildlife. Unfortunately, most of our major parks are already overpopulated with lodges and we shouldn't issue more licenses to build new ones in these main reserves. The government and Kenya Wildlife Service are looking into the possibility of opening up some of the older, less used parks. But some of the new lodges, like the one built by the Japanese on the bluff above the Mara River not far from Kichwa Tembo, are having trouble filling their eighty beds.

So much depends on the attitude of the Africans themselves. There is a great effort going on in all parts of Kenya and Africa as a whole to educate the general public about the value of wildlife. Beginning at the primary school level, we are trying to make this young generation aware of their wildlife heritage. I've got four kids. If there is hope for the wildlife and if my kids are directly or indirectly employed in tourism, they will have a chance not only to experience the wildlife, but to get their daily bread from it. That's just one of several reasons why I welcome the *Focus on Africa* project and am happy to donate my services as a guide.

TICH ATKINSON – *licensed hunter/guide and part owner of Musango Safari Camp in Zimbabwe*

Conservation of African wildlife boils down to money. If we can get people to understand that wildlife has value on a sustainable basis, they will want to look after that resource. The tribal people in the area have been killing the game for food for many years. If we can turn that game into a valuable resource—into schools and clinics and boreholes for water for the general benefit of the people in an area—this is probably the only way that the game is going to be preserved.

Operation CAMPFIRE is a scheme whereby the tribal people of an area are encouraged to understand that wildlife is a resource that can be utilized on a sustainable basis, whether for hunting or photographic safaris. It can be turned into dollars that can be used by the people to improve their standard of living. So far, Operation CAMPFIRE looks as if it's on track. The local people are realizing that the big game—lions, elephants, buffalo and so on—and the lease fees we pay for utilizing the area bring them definite benefits. They also find employment in the camp and that means wages that go back into the area...all as a result of the wildlife. However, if CAMPFIRE is not backed up by continuing support from the government and other authorities, it may flounder.

I believe that if hunting is properly controlled—overseen by qualified ecologists who are keeping close tabs on the system—a certain amount of the wildlife can safely be cropped. The dollars generated can then be turned back into wildlife conservation programs, but it does have to be very carefully controlled. And having professional hunters and guides out in the bush does have a deterrent effect on poachers. For example, not long ago I was out on a nature ramble with some of our guests. We had heard some lions calling early in the morning so we went to see what was happening. As we approached the area we found a poacher cutting up a dead lion. He had been after antelope and snared the lion accidentally. I arrested him and he's now serving time in jail.

The *Focus On Africa* project is a great idea because foreign exchange is probably the most important thing to these African countries with shaky economies. We have to be very careful that desire for dollars doesn't overtake the need to look after the environment—as we've seen in other countries in Africa—and over-commercialize or spoil it. It's a bit of a give and take situation. Nevertheless, tourism has to be and I believe will continue to be the most important single industry for us in Africa.

PATRICIA AWORI – *U.S. educated, B.A. in psychology and international relations, twenty-eight year association with wildlife, eleven as a professional guide*

I believe the *Focus On Africa* project will assist in bringing home to America the fact that there is a lot to be seen here, that it isn't dangerous, and why conservation is needed. Our world has become much more conservation-conscious and *Focus On Africa* will help in the same way the movie *Out Of Africa* did, by revealing just how much Africa has to offer.

Take the Masai Mara. It was established as a game reserve in 1953. The Mara has been perhaps the most popular game reserve we have in this country. For that reason the Maasai are becoming more involved in the management of the area so that they themselves can realize the benefits and ensure that it continues to be maintained in the future. Because people already know about the Mara, Amboseli, Tsavo, the Aberdares and Samburu, they tend to visit only those parks. Consequently, many lodges and permanent tented camps have been built there, increasing the volume of traffic in those particular parks tremendously. That has certainly resulted in some overcrowding and harassment of the wildlife, no doubt unintentionally in many cases because people don't always understand the consequences of their actions. The answer to such a problem, in my opinion, is to diversify. With more parks to visit and better informed people, we will have more responsible tourism.

When more money comes in and a better network of roads has been established in more of the parks, the problem of off-road driving will be alleviated, particularly in the Mara where the resulting damage is enormous. Getting everyone to obey the rules of off-road driving will require a major commitment from both the driver guides and the tourists, but with such a commitment we will have a better chance to ensure the survival of our wildlife.

There are over twenty lodges and tented camps in the Mara. They can accommodate a couple of thousand people who ride around in about five-hundred vehicles every day in a six-hundred square mile area. In the Serengeti's six-thousand square miles there are a few hundred beds.

There, they are careful about granting construction licenses and impose definite restrictions about where lodges can be built and how much bed space is allowed.

Even though it doesn't appear on too many organized tours, Meru National Park is, perhaps, a model for conservation. It has a brilliant network of roads, but it has only one lodge and that restricts the number of visitors. As a result, the park is principally used by small groups for which space can be guaranteed. Tour operators must start marketing other destinations more aggressively. Marsabit is one such place. We had a famous elephant called Ahmed with huge tusks that weighed more than 200 pounds apiece who once roamed Marsabit and people went there just to see him. But when Ahmed died, interest in Marsabit also died. We need to regenerate interest in Marsabit because the huge herds of elephants with big tusks that we just don't see on the plains any more are still to be found there.

When I heard about the *Focus On Africa* project and what it hoped to accomplish, I saw it as a wonderful forum in which to express how conservation can best be served. We are going through a terribly lean time in tourism—a lot of it because of negative publicity—and it was a pleasure indeed to hear that, finally, there was going to be some positive publicity. For example, the recent article by correspondent Paul Redfern in the *Nairobi Standard* on the damage tourists are allegedly doing to the wildlife failed to include, along with the tales of harassment of animals and so-called "sex tours," any of the more positive aspects of the situation.

I do not believe Kenya is a dangerous destination at all when you consider that we have had tourism in this country for almost a hundred years and have not had more than twenty tourist deaths, including road accidents, in all that time. When people are careless and wander off into the unknown unaccompanied, they are likely to have difficulties wherever they are. If you don't know how wildlife behaves, a problem could certainly arise, not just because the wildlife is dangerous, but because it may be looking for a way to protect itself in a situation that it finds threatening. If you are not conversant with the area and the animals, you may not realize that your behavior is threatening. Unfortunately, we don't have the best road system here. Breakdowns are liable to occur at any time and if you're not familiar with the area and are traveling alone you could find yourself in trouble. Taking a ranger with you only costs about two dollars a day and the difference could be enormous.

We here in Kenya cannot hope to ensure the future of wildlife by ourselves. It needs a global effort. We cannot maintain the wildlife without the money that comes from tourism and that is why a project like *Focus On Africa* is so important. If all these people come from so far away to see this, more Africans will realize that it must really be something important. The generation from which the future leaders of the country will come is very aware of the commercial value of tourism and the wildlife that brings it. If people really want to see what paradise is all about—get off the beaten path and truly appreciate God's creation—then they should go on safari. ✪

Where The Wild Things Are

Focus On Africa

Focus On Africa
visited eight countries: Botswana,
Kenya, Namibia, South Africa, Tanzania,
Zaire, Zambia, and Zimbabwe. Each is
regarded as a top destination for viewing
wildlife. Collectively, they offer habitat that
varies from the blistering red sands of the
Namib desert to the dense rainforests of
Zaire where the elusive and endangered
mountain and lowland gorillas live. To provide
background information and understanding,
each is briefly profiled below.

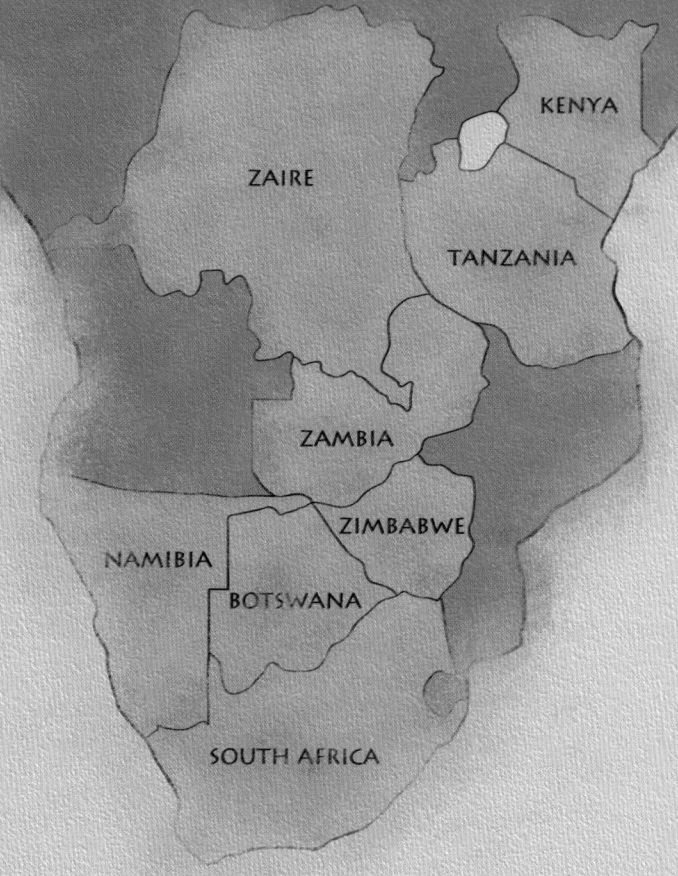

Botswana

Botswana, like all eight of the countries visited by *FOA*, is officially a Republic. Formerly known as Bechuanaland, it became Botswana— a name derived from the Tswana people—in 1966. Its capital is Gaborone. Most of its 231,805 square miles consist of the Kalahari desert. As of 1990, its estimated population stood at 1.3 million, more than three quarters of whom belong to eight Bantu-speaking ethnic groups, each with a tribal territory over which it holds inalienable communal ownership. The Kalahari is home to approximately 60,000 Bushmen (or San) whose ancestors may have arrived as many as 30,000 years ago. Their distinctive language includes unique clicking sounds. Botswana's only sources of permanent surface water are the rivers Chobe, Okavango and Limpopo. Rain falls erratically, resulting in frequent and sometimes protracted droughts and famines. The scarcity of water has kept Botswana sparsely populated, yet its birth rate is one of the highest in Africa. The full extent of the country's mineral resources remains unknown, but the Orapa, Lethakane and Jwaneng mines collectively contain one of the world's largest diamond reserves. Its economy has been heavily subsidized by South Africa, the EEC and other international agencies. Though still low by world standards, the growth rate of its GNP is among the highest in southern Africa.

Botswana's premier game-viewing areas lie in the Okavango Delta, Chobe National Park, the Moremi Wildlife Reserve, and Nxai Pan National Park, renowned for its enormous number of giraffe. All are concentrated in the north-central part of the country. Slightly less than half of the 7,900 square-mile Kalahari Gemsbok National Park, located in Botswana's southwestern corner, lies across the border in South Africa and can only be entered from that country. Some seventeen percent of Botswana has been set aside as parks and preserves. The combination of excellent game, uncrowded conditions, top quality small camps and open-vehicle game viewing make Botswana one of the best destinations in Africa.

Kenya

About the same size as Botswana, Kenya (224,961 square miles) has somehow come to represent Africa in a way that no other country quite does. Its capital, Nairobi, like the country itself, symbolizes the Africa that people associate with wildlife. Unfortunately, this very popularity has led to the overcrowded conditions in some of Kenya's most famous parks that have generated criticism of the ecological impact of tourism. Since it gained its independence in 1963, following the long and much publicized Mau Mau rebellion, its population has more than tripled. By 1990 it stood at nearly 25 million. Although its economic growth rate following independence was among the greatest in Africa, its even more rapidly expanding population outran the state's capacity to provide jobs, land, and social services. Its per capita GNP is among the continent's lowest.

The land, unlike mostly flat Botswana, contains five contrasting regions: the Lake Victoria basin; the Central Rift Highlands which are broken in two halves by the Rift Valley (the Mau Escarpment on the west and the Aberdare Range on the east); the Rift Valley itself;

the eastern plateau; and the 250 mile-long coastal belt with its famous port of Mombasa. Only about 4 percent of the land is suitable for farming and nearly all of that is planted in corn and other grains. In spite of this, however, Kenya's economy is largely based on agriculture which employs four fifths of the work force. Coffee and tea lead the list of exports, but the lion's share of foreign exchange comes from the tourist industry. The country has two rainy seasons: the so-called "long rains" from late March to May and the "short rains" from October to December.

Thirty to forty ethnic groups make up the population, chief among them the Kikuyu, Luhya, Luo, Kamba, Kalenjin and Maasai, distinguished from each other by both language and culture. Swahili and English are the official languages, but the various tribal tongues fall into the Bantu, Nilotic or Cushitic linguistic groups. The major game parks are Tsavo (East and West), Amboseli (best known for elephants and spectacular views of Mt. Kilimanjaro), Masai Mara (generally conceded to be the finest game reserve in Kenya), Samburu (with its distinctive reticulated giraffe, Grevy's zebra and gerenuk, found nowhere else), Nairobi (where you can see animals against a backdrop of the city skyline), Aberdare (with its famous treetop hotels), and Lake Nakuru (where the water is often pink with flamingos).

NAMIBIA

Like its eastern neighbor, Botswana, Namibia consists mostly of desert—the Namib, a parched and barren inferno of red sand dunes and rock outcroppings that runs for a thousand miles along the Atlantic coast, and the Kalahari. Between lies the more moderate Central Plateau. With 1.3 million people occupying 318,261 square miles, Namibia ranks as one of the least populated nations in the world. That's 4 people to the square mile, compared, for example, to Kenya's 111. On the other hand, it has been endowed with extensive deposits of valuable minerals such as diamonds, uranium, tin, tungsten, copper, manganese, lead, zinc, vanadium, lithium, limestone and rock salt. Not surprisingly, the economy depends almost entirely on mining and agriculture (the latter practiced mostly in the north). Until it achieved independence in 1990, Namibia was known as South West Africa. Its capital is Windhoek and English is the official language.

Namibia's history has been practically a textbook case of colonial rivalries at work. The German Rhenish Missionary Society arrived in the 1840s, but tribal wars impelled the Germans to offer the place to Britain in exchange for protection. Request denied... for the moment. In 1876, however, Britain did extend its colonial rule over the so-called Cape Colony, but not for long. Eight years later, Chancellor Otto von Bismarck finally offered complete German protection and then annexed the whole area. Soon, more tribal uprisings erupted among the Khoikhoin (Hottentots) and Herero. Shouldering the "white man's burden" in the era's usual way, the Germans responded by reducing the Herero from a tribe of 80,000 people to 15,000 starving refugees. With the discovery of diamonds in 1908, the European population grew predictably. During World War I, the Union of South Africa trounced the Germans and occupied South West Africa which was subsequently mandated to them by the short-lived League of Nations. In 1964, the United Nations voted to end South Africa's mandate, but South Africa resisted that decision and retained control of the country until 1988 when, after a long and bitter struggle with SWAPO guerrillas, they finally agreed to grant it independence.

Etosha National Park is Namibia's leading attraction and one of the world's largest parks. In Africa, it is exceeded in size only by its near-neighbor, Namib Naukluft and Zambia's Kafue. Remarkably, the park's 8,595 square miles are completely fenced, although this has little apparent effect on the peregrinations of the elephants. Apart from elephants, Etosha's fauna is immensely rich and varied, including more than 325 species of birds. Perhaps the most remarkable living thing in Namib Naukluft (which may be the world's oldest desert) is not an animal, but a plant—the astounding *Welwitschia mirabilis*. Like America's bristlecone pines, these strange "trees" live for thousands of years, making them among the oldest living things on earth. Skeleton Coast National Park, 2,000 square miles of dunes, canyons and mountains of the Namib desert, cannot compete with Etosha for large game viewing, yet shelters many small but fascinating creatures.

SOUTH AFRICA

South Africa has been consistently in the news for many years because of the long and bloody battle over its policy of enforced racial segregation called apartheid, first imposed in 1948. In May 1994, three centuries of white-minority rule came to an end when Nelson Mandela, after twenty seven years as one of history's most famous and influential political prisoners, became president in the country's first free election. The prelude to the election, like much of the recent past in South Africa, was marred by intertribal violence. Press coverage of such violence tends to discourage tourism. That is unfortunate because South Africa is far more than the sum of its internal political struggles. Among other unusual things, it has three separate capitals: an administrative one in Pretoria; a legislative one in Cape Town; and a judicial one in Bloemfontein. It also completely surrounds the small independent state of Lesotho (formerly Basutoland and pronounced Lesootoo), a geopolitical oddity that occurs in only two other places—the Vatican and the Republic of San Marino, both surrounded by Italy. Slightly more than 38 million people occupy South Africa's 471,445 square miles which are divided into three zones: the interior plateau, the surrounding Great Escarpment, and a narrow strip of coastal plain. Richly endowed with mineral resources, South Africa's gold and diamond mines have long been among its best known features. Even though gold's importance in the country's total mineral output has declined steadily since 1948, it still produces more of it than any other nation in the world. Such riches notwithstanding, growth of the GNP has not kept pace with the increase in population (no doubt due in part to the international economic sanctions imposed to induce the white regime to abandon apartheid). Even so, South Africa is, by a wide margin, the richest and most developed country in Africa.

The discovery of diamonds in 1868 and gold in 1886 brought boom times and an attempt by the British to sweep the Boer (Dutch for farmer) republics, Orange Free State and Transvaal, into a South African confederation. The Boers resisted, the British insisted and the Boer War of 1899 broke out, giving such youthful warriors as Winston Churchill an early experience of battle. By 1902, Boer resistance had been crushed and their republics annexed as new jewels in the British Crown Colonies. Eight years later the South African Act created the Union of South Africa.

South Africa has two major national parks: Kruger, second oldest park in Africa after Zaire's Virunga (originally called Albert) and Kalahari Gemsbok. Both are huge, although slightly more than half of Kalahari Gemsbok lies in Botswana. The story behind the creation of each says a great deal about the history of African wildlife conservation and the obstacles that confronted it in the early days. Just four years after Dutch Commander Jan van Riebeeck founded the settlement of Cape Town in 1652, he felt obliged to order restrictions on hunting because the wildlife, teeming when the settlers arrived, was already noticeably dwindling. By 1883, when Paul Kruger became President of the Transvaal Republic, the devastation had advanced apace. Kruger, a renowned hunter in his youth, underwent a conversion and shortly after assuming office proposed to the legislature (Volksrad) the creation of wildlife sanctuaries. The members greeted this radical notion as shocking religious heresy, but Kruger persevered and in 1898, against all odds, finally succeeded in establishing the Sabie Reserve. It became Kruger National Park in 1926 and, thanks largely to the tireless efforts of its first administrator, James Stevenson-Hamilton, eventually became the celebrated wildlife showplace it remains today.

The creation of Kalahari Gemsbok, on the other hand, recognized for the first time that animals cannot be expected to heed man-made political boundaries. When reserves were first created, at places where they should logically have spanned an international border they usually ended abruptly in a fence instead, cutting the animals off from what had for millions of years been their natural feeding ground. In Kalahari Gemsbok, the border was left open — an agreement that remained in place despite the profound political conflict that developed between Bechuanaland (Botswana) and South Africa.

TANZANIA

Consisting mostly of plains and plateau, Tanzania nevertheless possesses some superlative geographical features: The world's second deepest lake (Lake Tanganyika at 4,710 feet; only Siberia's Lake Baykal is deeper at 5,315); the world's second largest fresh water lake (26,828 square mile Lake Victoria, surpassed only by Lake Superior at 31,800) which it shares with Kenya and Uganda; Africa's highest point (Mt. Kilimanjaro, 19,340 feet, often erroneously presumed to be in Kenya because of the way it dominates Amboseli's scenery); the world's largest unbroken, unflooded caldera (Ngorongoro Crater, so lush it has been considered by some to be the original Garden of Eden); the continent's largest game reserve (the 22,000 square mile Selous, only a small part of which is open to the public); and a major portion of the Great Rift Valley, the world's greatest continental rift system. Tanzania's 364,900 square mile size is exceeded only by Zaire and South Africa among the eight countries visited by *FOA*. Almost half of its population of more than 24 million is less than 15 years old. Its birth rate puts it among the twelve fastest growing countries in the world, a distinction it shares with three other African nations: Kenya, Botswana and Libya. Tanzania's population consists of about 120 identifiable ethnic groups, none so numerous as to be dominant, and is among the least urbanized in Africa.

In the early years of the nineteenth century, trade in slaves and ivory dominated the region's economy. Sometime in the late 1840s, a pair of German missionaries sighted Mt. Kilimanjaro which, for some reason, aroused the interest of the German government. German colonists arrived in 1885 and, by 1907, Germany had established total control over the area. World War I changed all that when the British occupied the country which was later mandated to them by the League of Nations, marking yet another chapter in the European carving up of Africa. After World War II, Tanganyika became a United Nations trust territory and, in 1961, finally achieved independence and full admission to the U.N. It merged with the island of Zanzibar in 1964 to become the new republic of Tanzania. Founder and first president, Julius Nyerere, turned the new nation sharply left politically with the Arusha Declaration of 1967. His idealistic experiment in socialism, called *ujaama* (familyhood), eventually came unraveled when reality and human nature inevitably asserted themselves. Nyerere resigned as president in 1985. The new administration set the country on an altered course and began dismantling government control of the economy. The per capita GNP remains among the lowest in the world.

Some 95,000 square miles of Tanzania have been set aside as wildlife reserves — twenty-six percent of the entire country. The best known and most visited parks are Serengeti, Ngorongoro Crater and Lake Manyara, but others have much to offer as well, particularly since they tend to be less crowded. Among these are the relatively new Ruaha National Park, located in the south-central part of the country and almost as large as Serengeti; Gombe Stream National Park, made famous by Jane Goodall's study of the chimpanzees, on the northeastern shore of Lake Tanganyika; Tarangire National Park, southeast of Lake Manyara, noted for its grasslands dotted with grotesque baobab trees as well as its large elephant population; and Arusha National Park where most of the animals are forest-dwellers, making it one of the best places to see the striking black and white colobus monkeys. Mt. Kilimanjaro adds immensely to the backdrop in this tiny 53 square-mile park, just as it does in Kenya's Amboseli.

ZAIRE

In its checkered and often turbulent history, this country had been called the Congo Free State (1885-1908), the Belgian Congo (1908-1960), the Republic of the Congo (1960-1964), and the Democratic Republic of the Congo (1964-1971) before assuming its present name of Zaire. After Sudan and Algeria, it is the third largest nation in Africa with 905,568 square miles to contain its slightly more than 34 million people. All of its previous names derived, of course, from the magnificent 2,718 mile-long Congo River which ranks as the world's seventh longest and whose basin makes up three-fifths of the country's entire area. Here, in a rainforest second in extent only to the Amazon's, Tarzan's jungle Africa can be found.

Zaire is one of the world's top producers of cobalt and industrial diamonds and has significant reserves of high grade copper, but the per capita GNP, like Tanzania's, is among the world's lowest. On the other hand, it has about half of Africa's total hydroelectric output capacity. Its dependence on mineral exports leaves it vulnerable to international price fluctuations with concomitant effects on its foreign exchange. The country's few parks, while offering some of the continent's most intriguing and memorable experiences, are better suited to the more adventurous and are not heavily visited. Tourism is not a major source of foreign exchange.

Virunga National Park, which began life as Albert National Park, is the oldest in Africa, having been proclaimed by royal decree in 1925. Two of its main attractions are the lofty Ruwenzori (Mountains of the Moon) and the extremely endangered mountain gorillas.

However, these animals cannot be visited in pop-top vans; some hiking over rough and steep terrain is required. This and the limited visitor facilities have kept Virunga very uncrowded, but a recent decision by the EEC to upgrade everything in the park from accommodations to administration will probably change that. The almost indistinguishable lowland gorillas (slightly smaller, shorter-haired and living at lower altitudes than their mountain cousins) can be visited in the Kahuzi-Biega National Park, but reaching them requires a similar level of exertion. In both places, several gorilla families have been habituated to human visitors through the patient quotidian efforts of the guides charged with their protection. No one who experience a face-to-face encounter with a 450 pound silverback male gorilla of either species ever forgets it.

ZAMBIA

The recent history of Zambia and its southern neighbor, Zimbabwe, (formerly Northern and Southern Rhodesia respectively) represents the dying gasp of nineteenth century European colonialism and one of the final stages in the remaking of the map of Africa. Zambia—named for the Zambezi River that flows through its southern region and larger of the two countries—achieved independence when it seceded from the Central African Federation of Rhodesia and Nyasaland in 1963. About 8.5 million people live within its 290,586 square miles.

Cecil Rhodes and the British South Africa Company negotiated treaties with the Zambian chiefs in the 1890s after which the company administered the territory, named Northern Rhodesia in 1911, until 1924 when it became a British protectorate. A mining industry blossomed after the turn of the century, based largely on the so-called Copperbelt region of central Zambia where perhaps one sixth of the world's known copper reserves lie in beds of sandstone, shale and dolomite. The British South Africa Company held the mineral rights to these riches from 1924 until 1960, reaping all the profits while allowing the black Africans virtually no representation in the government. During the 1950s, however, strong winds of change began sweeping across the continent and the Africans began to take revolutionary steps to free themselves from the yoke of the white colonialist powers. Unfortunately, after Zambia achieved independence in 1964 the world price of copper began to decline. Since the country is heavily dependent on the mineral for foreign exchange, its balance of trade deteriorated. Further economic reverses occurred when sanctions were imposed against neighboring Rhodesia (Zimbabwe) in 1965. Throughout the 1970s, Zambia served as a refuge for guerrillas fighting independence wars in Angola, Mozambique, Rhodesia and South Africa. Many white South African farmers left the country to escape the internal turmoil and what they probably saw as the inescapable outcome, causing a decline in agricultural production as well. Today, its population growth rate is among the highest in sub-Saharan Africa and, like Tanzania's, nearly half is less than 15 years old.

With nineteen national parks and thirty-four game management areas adjacent to them, Zambia has set aside an astounding thirty- two percent of its land for the preservation of wildlife. However, the general public is not admitted to many of these parks and reserves. Best of those that are open to the public are North and South Luangwa and Kafue National Parks. South Luangwa has been the most popular because of its large concentration of elephants and other game and because in Kafue, even though it is more than twice South Luangwa's size (8,648 square miles to 3,494), game is harder to see because of the dense forest with which much of it is clothed. Kafue is, however, one of the very few places where herds of the rare red lechwe antelope can be seen. In North Luangwa, Mark and Delia Owens—researchers and tireless campaigners on behalf of wildlife who chronicled their experiences in *Cry of the Kalahari* and *The Eye of the Elephant*—have been working for several years to stop the rampant poaching and build an infrastructure to attract tourists. In Zambia, visitors aren't just whisked around from place to place in vans; they are encouraged to get closer to the wildlife on walking, night, and boat safaris that greatly enhance the experience. No trip to Zambia should fail to include a visit to the awesome Victoria Falls (Mosi-oa-Tunya—"the smoke that thunders"), one of the world's most impressive and beautiful displays of the raw power of water.

ZIMBABWE

The name Zimbabwe comes from the Bantu word for "stone dwelling"—a good choice because the ruins of Great Zimbabwe, southeast of Nyanda (formerly Fort Victoria), are among its most intriguing landmarks. From the 11th to the 15th century, Great Zimbabwe apparently functioned as a center—perhaps religious—of a huge inland empire ruled by people known as the Karanga, but despite much archaeological research, the origin of the ruins remains a mystery. Immensely old, this vast complex of stone structures covers more than sixty acres and appears to have been occupied since the 2nd century AD, but no one really knows who by. The fact that they were built with stone makes them distinctly anomalous in a land where most structures have traditionally been composed of mud, cow dung and straw. Odder still, the stones stay in place without any kind of mortar. The ruins were discovered by settlers in 1898.

About half the size of Zambia, Zimbabwe (150,804 square miles) has a slightly larger population of 9.3 million of whom the vast majority are the Shona (70%) and the Ndebele (16%). The population is growing fast, although not so fast as many other African countries. The economy, more diversified than most in sub-Saharan Africa, probably benefited more than it suffered from the sanctions imposed on it by the outside world from 1965 to 1980 since they forced it to become largely self-sufficient. The sanctions, begun by England and later joined by the U.N., grew out of the white Rhodesian Front government's unilateral decision to terminate its status as a British colony. Tourism has had its ups and downs, falling to almost nil during the civil war of the late 1970s, rising sharply in 1980, plummeting again when hostilities broke out between the Shona and the Ndebele, reviving again in the mid eighties.

Zimbabwe's parks, particularly the three generally accepted as its best—Hwange, Matusadona and Mana Pools—are well-maintained and offer excellent and varied game viewing. In fact, Zimbabwe offers more ways to see animals than any other country in Africa, including day and night game drives in open vehicles, walking safaris, white-water rafting, canoeing, kayaking, and houseboating... something to suit every taste. To make all this even more appealing, Air Zimbabwe has daily flights that connect Victoria Falls, Hwange, Kariba and other points near the parks, thus eliminating the necessity, for those who can take advantage of them, of spending long hours on the road.

African Sponsors

Abercrombie & Kent, Ltd.
P.O. Box 59749, Nairobi, Kenya

Abercrombie & Kent Tanzania, Ltd.
P.O. Box 427, Arusha, Tanzania

Africa Calls, Ltd.
Box 22, Mfuwe, Zambia

African Pride Tours
21 Airlie Road, Bergvliet 7945
Cape Town, South Africa

African Tours & Hotels, Ltd.
P.O. Box 30472, Nairobi, Kenya
Mountain Lodge
Kilaguni Lodge
Olkurruk Mara Lodge

Block Hotels
P.O. Box 40075, Nairobi, Kenya
Lake Naivasha Country Club
Samburu Game Lodge
Keekorok Lodge
The Indian Ocean Beach Club
Nyali Beach Hotel
Larsens Camp
Treetops

Chinzombo Safaris
P.O. Box 30106, Lusaka, Zambia
Chinzombo Safari Lodge

Chizarira Lodge
P.O. Box 18, Victoria Falls, Zimbabwe

Cutty Sark Hotel
P.O. Box 80, Kariba, Zimbabwe

Cybele Forest Lodge
P.O. Box 346, White River 1240
South Africa

Delamere Camps, Ltd.
P.O. Box 48019, Nairobi, Kenya

Destination Africa
P.O. Box 59749, Nairobi, Kenya

Etendeke Mountain Camp
P.O. Box 34, Kamanjab, Namibia 9000

Giraffe Manor/African Fund for Endangered Wildlife, Inc.
P.O. Box 15004, Langata, Nairobi, Kenya

Hilton International
P.O. Box 30624, Nairobi, Kenya
Nairobi Hilton
Taita Hills Safari Lodge

Ilala Lodge
P.O. Box 18, Victoria Falls, Zimbabwe

Kapani Safari Lodge
P.O. Box 100, Mfuwe, Zambia

Ker & Downey
13201 NW Freeway, Suite 850
Houston, Texas 77040
Camp Serengeti South
Camp Serengeti Mara
Abu's Camp
Pom Pom
Shinde Island Camp
Machaba

Khorixas Rest Camp
P.O. Box 2, Khorixas, Namibia 9000

Kilimanjaro Safari Club
P.O. Box 30139, Nairobi, Kenya
Amboseli Lodge

Kiwayu Safari Village, Ltd.
P.O. Box 55343, Nairobi, Kenya

Kwabhekithunga
P.O. Box 364
Eshowe, 3875, South Africa

Lianshulu Lodge
P.O.Box 142, Katima Mulilo, Namibia

Lilayi Lodge
P.O. Box 30093, Lusaka, Zambi

Lonrho Hotels Kenya, Ltd.
P.O. Box 58581, Nairobi, Kenya
The Aberdare Country Club
Mount Kenya Safari Club
Ol Pejeta Ranch House
The Ark
The Norfolk Hotel

Masai Mara River Camp
P.O. Box 48019, Nairobi, Kenya

Mayana Lodge
P.O. Box 144, Kambat, Namibia 9000

Motswari/M'bali Private Game Reserve
P.O. Box 67865, Bryanston 2021
South Africa

Mount Sheba Lodge
P.O. Box 100, Pilgrims Rest 1290
South Africa

Msasa Safaris, Ltd.
P.O. Box 32575, Lusaka, Zambia

Musango Safari Camp
P.O. Box UA306, Harare, Zimbabwe

Musiara, Ltd.
P.O. Box 48217, Nairobi, Kenya
Governors' Camp

Namib Wilderness Safaris
P.O. Box 6850, Windhoek, Namibia 9000

Nature Conservation/Namibia Tourism
Pvt. Bag 13346, Windhoek, Namibia 9000

Ndutu Safari Lodge
P.O. Box 2, Karatu, Tanzania

Ngorongoro Safari Lodge, Ltd.
P.O. Box 2, Karatu, Tanzania
Gibb's Farm

Okavango Wilderness Safaris (Pty.) Ltd.
Pvt. Bag 14, Maun, Botswana
Mokoro Trails Camp
Mombo Camp
Jedibe Island Camp

Ongava Lodge
P.O. Box 186, Outjo, Namibia 9000

Orchids' Safari Club
B.P. 961, Bukavu, Zaire

Peponi Hotel
P.O. Box 24, Lamu, Kenya

Phinda Resource Reserve
P.O.Box 1211, Sunninghill Park 2157
South Africa

Prestige Hotels, Ltd.
P.O. Box 74888, Nairobi, Kenya
Samburu Intrepids Club
Mara Intrepids Club

Robin Pope Safaris
P.O. Box 320154, Lusaka, Zambia
Tena Tena

Sabi Sabi Game Reserve
P.O. Box 52665, Saxonwold 2132
South Africa

Safari Hotel
P.O. Box 3900, Windhoek, Namibia 9000

Safari Park Hotel
P.O. Box 45038, Nairobi, Kenya

Sarova Hotels
P.O. Box 30680, Nairobi, Kenya
Sarova Mara
Sarova Shaba

Savuti Allan's Camp
P.O. Box 100, Maun, Botswana

Savuti South Camp
P.O. Box 100, Maun, Botswana

Serena Lodges & Hotels
P.O. Box 48690, Nairobi, Kenya
Nairobi Serena Hotel
Samburu Serena Lodge
Mara Serena Lodge
Amboseli Serena Lodge

Serengeti Select Safaris, Ltd.
P.O. Box 2703, Arusha, Tanzania
Tarangire Safari Lodge

Sopa Lodges
P.O. Box 72630 Nairobi, Kenya
Ngorongoro Sopa Lodge
Serengeti Sopa Lodge
Mara Sopa Lodge

Swakopmund Bungalows/Swakop Municipality
Pvt. Bag 5017, Swakopmund
Namibia 9000

Tongabezi
Pvt. Bag 31, Livingstone, Zambia
Tongabezi Lodge
Sindabezi Island Camp

Touch the Wild Safaris
Pvt. Bag 6, Hillside, Bulawayo, Zimbabwe
Matobo Hills Lodge
Sikumi Tree Lodge
Makalolo Tented Camp

Ulusaba Game Lodge
P.O. Box 785368, Sandton 2146
South Africa

Wilderness Safaris
P.O.Box 651171, Benmore 2010
South Africa
Rocktail Bay Lodge

Wilderness Safaris Zimbabwe
P.O. Box 288, Victoria Falls, Zimbabwe

Wilderness Trails (K), Ltd.
P.O. Box 56923, Nairobi, Kenya
Lewa Downs

Windsor Hotels, International
P.O. Box 74957, Nairobi, Kenya
Mt. Meru Game Lodge,
Ngorongoro Crater Lodge
Windsor Golf and Country Club
Siana Springs
Kichwa Tembo

Zambia River Safaris
P.O. Box 30050, Lusaka, Zambia

Zimbabwe Sun Hotels
P.O. Box 8221, Causeway, Harare,
Zimbabwe
Bulawayo Sun Hotel
Elephant Hills
Bumi Hills Safari Lodge

AMERICAN SPONSORS

Brooks Institute of Photography
801 Alston Road
Santa Barbara, California 93108

Canon U.S.A., Inc.
One Canon Plaza
Lake Success, New York 11042

David Anderson Safaris
3463 State Street, Suite 403
Santa Barbara, California 93105

Eastman Kodak Company
343 State Street
Rochester, New York 14650

Lowepro
2194 Northpoint Parkway
Santa Rosa, California 95407

Outdoor Photographer Magazine
12121 Wilshire Blvd., 12th Floor
Los Angeles, California 90025

South African Airways
900 Third Avenue
New York, New York 10022

Victor Hasselblad Inc.
10 Madison Road
Fairfield, New Jersey 07004

Willis & Geiger, Inc.
36 W. Forty Fourth Street
New York, New York 10036

ACKNOWLEDGEMENTS

Few people realize that it takes almost as many people to make a project like *Focus On Africa* into a reality as it does to make a major motion picture. Watching the credits roll at the end of a feature film, there's hardly time to read all the names, let alone grasp what part each of the people may have played in the production. How many know or care what a "best boy" or a "key grip" does? The audience often drifts away and the crew's contribution to the entertainment goes unnoted. In books, too, probably few readers take the time to peruse the list of people who made it all possible—except, of course, the people themselves. For them, therefore, and for anyone else who might be interested or just looking for a familiar name, *Focus On Africa* wishes to express its gratitude to all who generously contributed their help in so many different ways. In any complex endeavor such as this, certain individuals' efforts extend well beyond the ordinary. In that category and meriting our special thanks and recognition are:

Julie de Kock and Mary Jane Headlee Clevenger, for their heroic and indefatigable efforts in getting us all to Africa and back with a minimum of flap and fiasco; Ruth Verbois, for keeping us on course with her flawless management and organization of the myriad pieces to the puzzle; Ralph Clevenger, for his invaluable assistance in helping us to sort through mountains of photo submissions and, with his wife Mary Jane's help, to identify all the animals, proofread the text and picture captions and otherwise provide all-around general support; Shukri Farhad, for technical assistance and expertise that extended his company's name of Newforce, Inc. to a new level of meaning; Jeff Litherland of Media 27, Inc., who gave generously of his free time in preparing the high-resolution scans; the entire crew at Freelance Graphics, for their unstinting way-beyond-the-call prepress handling of the flood we unleashed on them; Cheryl Opperman, for her legal work and marketing campaign; Gail Anderson, for general coordination at David Anderson Safaris; Chalermpon Poungpeth (known to his colleagues as "Yo") of the Brooks Institute Computer Lab, for his expert help making color prints of layouts; Arledge Armenaki of Brooks Institute, for his documentary film work; Farid Suleiman, Patricia Awori, Lynn Leakey, Ambrose Gachui, Gerald Selempo and Mohammed Saleh, professional guides who willingly donated their vital and illuminating services to our Kenya safaris; Trevor Hewett of African Pride Tours, South Africa, for assisting with all the necessary extras in that part of the continent; Duncan Muriuki and Peter Kiura of Destination Africa, Kenya, for performing the monumental chore of coordinating everything in East Africa; Babette Alfieri of Africa Calls, Zambia, for her indispensable help in opening Zambian doors; Jonathan Scott, for taking the time to address the *Focus On Africa* group at the opening of the project in Nairobi; Maasai village chief Ben Kipeno, for giving us an intimate look at his people's way of life; Rose Mburu of Abercrombie & Kent Explorations, Zaire, for rescuing one of our gorilla-trekking safaris when we had to redirect it from Rwanda to Zaire at the last minute; Colin Church of Church, Orr & Associates for his assistance with news releases in Kenya; Pony Eagleton, Dorothy Kuhne and June Shipley for patient, painstaking proofreading to prevent pratfalls; and finally, Skip Cohen, President of Victor Hasselblad Inc., for leading the way among our corporate sponsors in wholeheartedly supporting the project.

To all the others whose names would fill a book on their own, we extend our deep appreciation and thanks for a job well done.

Photo Credits

Page 7 David Johnson; **8** Raymond Watt; **9** Barry Bartolacci; **10** Michael Verbois; **36** Ralph Clevenger; **38** Robert Fairbanks; **40** Dorothy Kuhne; *inset, left and right* - Maxine Valdez; Larry White; **42** Peter Caine; **44** David Anderson; **45** *left, top and center* - Gene Davis; *bottom* - Sharon Hackley; *center, top to bottom* - Marilyn Iannarelli; Sharon Hackley; *right, top to bottom* - David Anderson; Janice Bartlett; **46** Cheryl Opperman; **47** *top to bottom* - Portia Racasi; David Anderson; David Bridge; **48** David Johnson; **50** Rob Cushman; **52/53** *bottom* - Daphne Polson; *inset left to right* - David Anderson; Raymond Watt; Jay Thamert; **54/55** Michael Verbois; **56** *top* - David Anderson; *center and bottom* - Michael Verbois; *strip* - Ralph Clevenger; **57** *top* - Ruth Verbois; *center inset and bottom* - David Anderson; **58** *top* - Ralph Clevenger; *left, bottom* - David Anderson; *center and right, bottom* - Michael Verbois; **59** Peter Caine; **60** Michael Verbois; **61** *left to right, top* - David Anderson; Tim Allen; Raimar Richers; *bottom* - David Anderson; **62/63** Michael Verbois; **64** *top to bottom* - Paula Adams; David Anderson; Ralph Clevenger; **65** Mark Van Bergh; **66** Michael Verbois; **67** *top and bottom* - Jay Thamert; **68** Mary Patton; **69** Nancy Nevin; **70/71** David Anderson; **72/73** Michael Verbois; **74** *top to bottom* - Virginia Rider; Donna Hands; Ralph Clevenger; **75** Ralph Clevenger; **76** Paul Lee; **78** *left, top to bottom* - Raymond Watt; Brian Hastings; David Anderson; David Soong; David Soong; *right* - Michael Verbois; **79** Michael Verbois; **80** Jessie Harris; **81** *left, top to bottom* - Sylvia Hosie; David Johnson; *right, top to bottom* - Jessie Harris; Gail Anderson; **82/83** Cheryl Opperman; **82** *inset, top to bottom* - Ruth Verbois; Ralph Clevenger; David Bridge; Ralph Clevenger; David Bridge; **84** *top to bottom* - Michael Verbois; David Bridge; Ron Berchin; Ruth Verbois; **85** David Bridge; **86** Donna Hands; **87** *top to bottom* - Ruth Verbois; Cheryl Opperman; Mark Van Bergh; **88** David Johnson; **89** David Anderson; **90** Michael Verbois; **91** *top and bottom* - Michael Verbois; *center* - David Anderson; **92** Mark Van Bergh; **93** *top* - David Bridge; remainder by Michael Verbois; **94** Donna Hands; **95** Michael Verbois; **96** *top to bottom* - Michael Verbois; David Anderson; Dorothy Kuhne; Paul Lee; Ralph Clevenger; remainder by Michael Verbois; **97** *top to bottom* - Mark Van Bergh; Michael Verbois; Ruth Verbois; Michael Verbois; Charles Graham; Cheryl Opperman; David Anderson; **98** *top and bottom* - Michael Verbois; *center* - David Soong; **99** Michael Verbois; **100** *large image* - Ralph Clevenger; *insets, top to bottom* - Dorothy Kuhne; David Anderson; Daphne Polson; Joseph Denker; **101** *top to bottom* - Barry Bartolacci; Rob Cushman; David Johnson; David Anderson; **102** Michael Verbois; *insets, left to right* - Michael Verbois; Rob Cushman; **104** Michael Verbois; **105** *top to bottom* - Carlo Quaia; Jay Thamert; Kelly Stone; **106** David Johnson; **108** Rob Cushman; **109** *top and center* - Michael Verbois; *bottom* - David Anderson; **110** *top, left to right* - Edward Morris; David Anderson; *bottom* - Andrew Horton; **111** *top, left to right* - David Anderson; Edward Morris; **112** David Anderson; **114** *left to right* - Michael Verbois; David Bridge; **115** David Bridge; **116** Judy Ozmar; **118** *top* - Dorothy Kuhne; *bottom* - David Anderson; **120** *left insets, top to bottom* - David Anderson; following two by Raymond Watt; David Anderson; Raymond Watt; **120/121** Raymond Watt; **122/123** David Anderson; **124** *left, top and bottom* - Donna Hands; Janet Gorski; *right bottom* - Mary Jane Sesto; **125** Michael Verbois; **126** *left, top to bottom* - Barry Bartolacci; David Bridge; Michael Verbois; *right, top to bottom* - Brian Hastings; Larry White; Barry Bartolacci; **127** *left, top to bottom* - David Friedner; Barry Bartolacci; Carlo Quaia; *right, top to bottom* - Jessie Harris; Barry Bartolacci; Charles Gutierrez; **128** David Anderson; **129** *top to bottom* - Charles Graham; Mary Jane Headlee Clevenger; David Anderson; **130** *top and bottom* - Sharon Hackley; **131** Ralph Clevenger; **132** Ralph Clevenger; **134** *top to bottom* - Charles Gutierrez; following two by Michael Verbois; Rob Cushman; **135** Michael Verbois; **136/137** David Anderson; *insets, left to right* - Andrew Horton; Dorothy Kuhne; Michael Verbois; **138** *top to bottom* - Preston Ozmar; Donna Hands; **139** Mark Van Bergh; **140/141** Anya Cristina Stout; **142** *top to bottom* - Ruth Verbois; David Anderson; Rob Cushman; **143** David Anderson; **144** Michael Verbois; **145** Karen McGougan; **146/147** Gail Anderson; *insets, left to right* - Brian Hastings; Herb Lundin; Mary Jane Sesto; Jessie Harris; **148/149** Sylvia Hosie; **150** David Anderson **151** *top and bottom* - Anya Cristina Stout; **152** David Anderson; **154** David Anderson; **155** Ellen Silbermann; **156** *top to bottom* - Peter Caine; Michael Verbois; **157** Peter Caine; **158/159** Mark Van Bergh; **160** Anya Cristina Stout; **161** *top to bottom* - Samuel Saylor; Peter Caine; Michael Verbois; **162** *top to bottom* - Michael Verbois; Glenna Evans; Peter Caine; **163** Rob Cushman; **164** *left, top to bottom* - Michael Verbois; Ralph Clevenger; Cheryl Opperman; *right, top to bottom* - Carlo Quaia; Peter Caine; Daphne Polson; **165** *left, top to bottom* - Cheryl Opperman; Ralph Clevenger; Judy Ozmar; *right, top and bottom* - Barry Bartolacci; *center* - Natalie Brecher; **166** *top to bottom* - Jessie Harris; Steve Welsh; David Anderson; **167** Michael Verbois; **168** David Johnson; **169** *top to bottom* - Maxine Valdez; Donna Hands; **170** *left, top to bottom* - Portia Racasi; David Anderson; Michael Verbois; *right* - Natalie Brecher; **171** Ruth Verbois; **172** Paul Lee; **173** *left, top* - Michael Verbois; *center and bottom* - Rob Cushman; *right, top to bottom* - David Johnson; Raymond Watt; Daphne Polson; **174** Ralph Clevenger; **176** Mark Van Bergh; **177** Michael Verbois; **178** Ralph Clevenger; **179** *top to bottom* - Brian Hastings; Michael Verbois; **180** Brian Hastings; **181** *top to bottom* - Raymond Kammer; David Anderson; following three by Raymond Watt; **182** *top and bottom* - Raymond Watt; **183** Karen Vernon; **184** *left, top and center* - Susan Peterson; *bottom* - Richard Jarvi; *right, top to bottom* - Richard Jarvi; David Soong; Nancy McCarthy; **185** Nancy McCarthy; **186** Ruth Verbois; **187** *insets, left to right* - David Bridge; Richard Nunley; **188/189** *left* - Michael Verbois; *center, top to bottom* - David Soong; Mark Van Bergh; *right* - Robert Fairbanks; **190** Ralph Clevenger; **195** Ralph Clevenger; **206** *left, top to bottom* - Ralph Clevenger; Paul Lee; David Anderson; Ruth Verbois; Mark Evans; Barry Bartolacci; *center, top to bottom* - Diane Henderson; David Bridge; Ralph Clevenger; Ralph Clevenger; David Anderson; David Anderson; *right, top to bottom* - David Anderson; Sylvia Hosie; David Anderson; Raymond Watt; Raymond Watt; David Anderson; **207** *left, top to bottom* - Michael Verbois; Ralph Clevenger; David Anderson; Michael Verbois; Raymond Watt; Ruth Verbois; *center, top to bottom* - Raymond Watt; David Anderson; David Anderson; Michael Verbois; David Anderson; Raymond Watt; *right, top to bottom* - David Anderson; Raymond Watt; David Anderson; David Anderson; Karen McGougan; Ruth Verbois; **208** David Anderson; **209** Michael Verbois; **210** *left* - David Anderson; *right* - David Bridge; **218** *left, top to bottom* - David Anderson; Michael Verbois; Anya Cristina Stout; Barry Bartolacci; Brian Hastings; Michael Verbois; *center, top to bottom* - Ralph Clevenger; David Anderson; Brian Hastings; Ralph Clevenger; David Anderson; Gene Davis; *right, top to bottom* - Peter Caine; David Anderson; Judy Ozmar; David Anderson; Michael Verbois; Ron Berchin; **219** *left, top to bottom* - Steve Welsh; David Bridge; Barry Bartolacci; Edmond Alexander; Ralph Clevenger; Ralph Clevenger; *center, top to bottom* - David Soong; Gail Molzahn; David Anderson; Ed Snoke; Portia Racasi; Brian Hastings; *right, top to bottom* - Michael Verbois; Brian Hastings; David Anderson; Brian Hastings; David Bridge; Raymond Watt; **220** *left, top to bottom* - Charles Gutierrez; Donna Hands; David Anderson; Charles Gutierrez; Ralph Clevenger; Ann Stanley; *center, top to bottom* - David Bridge; David Anderson; Michael Verbois; Donna Hands; Donna Hands; Ralph Clevenger; *right, top to bottom* - Brian Hastings; David Anderson; David Johnson; Brian Hastings; Preston Ozmar; David Anderson; **221** *left, top to bottom* - Michael Verbois; Donna Hands; Ralph Clevenger; Carlo Quaia; Dorothy Kuhne; Janet Gorski; *center, top to bottom* - Brian Hastings; Marvin Jetton; following two by David Anderson; Edward Morris; Peter Caine; *right, top to bottom* - Ralph Clevenger; Peter Caine; Nancy McCarthy; Portia Racasi; Michael Verbois; David Anderson; **224** Portia Racasi

Bibliography and suggested additional reading

Amin, Mohamed; Willetts, Duncan; Tetley, Brian. *Journey Through Kenya.* Nairobi: Camerapix, 1982

Balfour, Daryl & Sharna. *Etosha.* Cape Town, South Africa: Struik Publishers, 1992

Bechky, Allen. *Adventuring in East Africa.* San Francisco: Sierra Club Books, 1990

Beston, Henry. *The Outermost House.* New York: Penguin, 1928

Bonner, Raymond. *At The Hand of Man: Peril and Hope for Africa's Wildlife.* New York: Alfred E. Knopf, 1993. Excerpts from *At The Hand of Man: Peril and Hope for Africa's Wildlife* © Raymond Bonner, reprinted by permission of Random House, Inc. All rights reserved.

Churchill, Winston S. *My African Journey.* London: Hodder & Stoughton, 1908. New York: W.W. Norton & Co., Inc., reprint 1990

Dinesen, Isak. *Out Of Africa.* New York: Random House, 1937

Ehrlich, Paul R. *The Population Bomb.* New York: Ballantine Books, 1968

Fossey, Dian. *Gorillas In The Mist.* Boston: Houghton Mifflin Company, 1983

Goodall, Jane. *My Friends, The Wild Chimpanzees.* Washington, D.C.: National Geographic Society, 1967

Gordon, René. *Africa: A Continent Revealed.* Cape Town, South Africa: Struik Publishers, 1980

Grzimek, Bernhard. *Serengeti Shall Not Die.* London: Collins, reprint 1978

Haltendorth, Theodor & Diller, Helmut. *Mammals of Africa.* London: William Collins Sons & Co. Ltd., 1986

Hes, Lex. *The Leopards of Londolozi.* Cape Town, South Africa: Struik Publishers, Ltd., 1991

Künkel, Reinhard. *Elephants.* New York: Harry N. Abrams, Inc., 1983

Künkel, Reinhard. *Ngorongoro.* New York: Harry N. Abrams, Inc., 1993

Lanting, Frans. *Okavango: Africa's Last Eden.* San Francisco: Chronicle Books, 1993

Larousse. *The Larousse Encyclopedia of Animal Life.* New York: McGraw Hill, 1967

Leakey, Richard E. & Lewin, Roger. *Origins.* New York: E.P. Dutton, 1977

Luard, Nicholas. *The Wildlife Parks of Africa.* Salem, New Hampshire: Salem House, 1986

Markham, Beryl. *West With The Night.* New York: Houghton Mifflin Company, 1942

Matthiessen, Peter. *The Tree Where Man Was Born.* New York: Donadio & Ashworth, Inc. 1972. Excerpts from pages 148, 124 and 151 of *The Tree Where Man Was Born,* © Peter Matthiessen, reprinted by permission of Donadio & Ashworth, Inc. All rights reserved.

Moorehead, Alan. *No Room In The Ark.* New York: Harper & Bros., 1959

Moss, Cynthia. *Elephant Memories.* New York: William Morrow & Co., Inc., 1988. Excerpt from *Elephant Memories* © Cynthia Moss, reprinted by permission of William Morrow & Co., Inc. All rights reserved.

Moss, Cynthia. *Portraits in the Wild.* Chicago: University of Chicago Press, 1975

Nolting, Mark W. *Africa's Top Wildlife Countries.* Pompano Beach, Florida: Global Travel Publishers, Inc., 1990

Owens, Delia & Mark. *The Eye of the Elephant.* New York: Houghton Mifflin Company, 1992. Excerpt from *The Eye of the Elephant* © Delia and Mark Owens, reprinted by permission of Houghton Mifflin Company. All rights reserved.

Owens, Delia & Mark. *Cry of the Kalahari.* New York: Houghton Mifflin Company, 1984

Parker, Ian & Amin, Mohamed. *Ivory Crisis.* London: Chatto & Windus Ltd., 1983

Roosevelt, Theodore. *African Game Trails.* New York: Scribner, 1910

Schaller, George. *The Year of the Gorilla.* Chicago: University of Chicago Press, 1964

Scott, Jonathan. *The Leopard's Tale.* London: Elm Tree Books, 1985

Selous, Frederick Courteney. *Travel & Adventure In Southeast Africa,* 1881. North Pomfret, VT., Trafalgar Square, reprint 1988

Williams, J.G. & Arlott, N. *Birds of East Africa.* London: William Collins Sons & Co. Ltd., 1986